PUBLIC PEOPLE, PRIVA

Public People, Private Lives

Tackling Stress in Clergy Families

Jean and Christopher Burton

continuum

Published by Continuum

The Tower Building　　　　　80 Maiden Lane
11 York Road　　　　　　　　Suite 704
London　　　　　　　　　　　New York
SE1 7NX　　　　　　　　　　　NY 10038

www.continuumbooks.com

First published 2009

British Library Cataloguing-in-Publication Data
A catalogue record for this book is available from the British Library.

ISBN 9780826426123

Typeset by BookEns Ltd., Royston, Herts.
Printed and bound in Great Britain by the MPG Books Group

For our sons Mark and Tim

*who shared with us the rollercoaster road of clergy family life
with such humour, patience and support*

Contents

Acknowledgements

First and foremost we would like to thank the Trusts who supported our research: The Ecclesiastical Insurance Group's Bursary Awards, The Jerusalem Trust, The Archbishop of Canterbury's Discretionary Fund, The Trebor Trust and especially the Neville Russell Trust which was our main sponsor. Without their generosity the research on which this book is based would not have been possible.

The particular group to whom we owe an enormous debt must, for reasons of confidentiality, remain anonymous. They are the families and members of the two Reference groups at the heart of our research who took part in the three sets of interviews and group meetings, over such an extended period of time, with great commitment, openness and goodwill.

We received endless wise guidance from our tutors at Bristol University, Professor Phyllida Parsloe and Dr Brian Caddick. Their constant encouragement smoothed the path of such an extensive project. Our family therapy consultant, Ros Draper, brought her long experience to our discussions as we framed the interviews and questions.

We learned so much from friends old and new who offered us hospitality in the United States when we explored the American clergy experience at the beginning of our research. The friends with whom we stayed in different parts of this country while we carried out our interviews were a special part of the whole process.

The deep well of experience of the late Dr Hugh Tollinton and Geraldine Tollinton, as psychiatrist and psychologist respectively, fed much into our thinking and understanding as we analysed our data. Angela and Tony Bushell and Penny Peerless offered us the space and hospitality we needed at the crucial final writing stages. Olga Levitt gave us much support and also helped us to realize the relevance of our work for the families of rabbis. We have valued their friendship, care and support over many years.

Those who have turned an academic thesis into a book will appreciate particularly the skill and patience of those who helped us to convert not one, but two, theses into Public People, Private Lives. Our special thanks, therefore, go to Matthew Dieppe, Peter Jones, Virginia Hearn and Professor John Shack in Chicago for reading the different drafts and for all that they contributed to make the book a reality. Our managing editor at Continuum, Caroline Chartres, has given us warm support and guidance for the final stages of producing the book.

The practical and technical expertise generously given at key moments by John Winterbotham, David and Alison Palmer, Geoff Dodgson, Karen Salter and Rosalind Moran has been invaluable.

We are deeply grateful to them all.

Preface

The content of this book is shocking and at the same time inspiring. Although it is written in the cool prose of an academic study, the muted and anonymous accounts, given by the Anglican clergy families of the situations in which they live, are startling and shaming. From the time of entering theological college, and certainly following ordination, most clergy families move frequently and these moves don't necessarily suit the needs of children taking exams, of working wives or elderly parents. Often the cleric appears to be treated as if he were an individual unit, called to meet the needs of the Church. Children suffer from loss of friends on top of the sad and seemingly inevitable disadvantages of being a clergy child amongst their peers. Nor are the moves always made easy by the congregation; we could make such a difference, but often do not.

Not owning the house which is their temporary home is a constant worry not least for the children, as the comment by one small child showed when saying it would better for Mummy to die first because they would then have a house. It is less certain that they actually would, since many clergy made clear they did not think they could go on in the job without their wives.

But the account is also inspiring. The obvious question for me is why do these families put up with this difficult life? The answer is the faith and commitment of the couples. How fortunate the people of the Church of England are to have such faith and commitment in their clergy families – it is more than we deserve. I only hope that since this research took place things have at least begun to improve. Congregations now have a much larger role in the financial support of their clergy which could be a force for good.

Jean and Chris make suggestions for change, based on their extensive research. Many of their recommendations depend upon action by senior people in the Church, whose lives did not form part of the research, but the comments from the groups with whom the Burtons discussed their findings suggest that these leaders probably live equally stressful and difficult lives. The book hints that new entrants to the ministry may not accept the kind of conditions which the research families disclosed. I wonder whether women priests take a different stance when trying to balance the needs of their vocation against those of their husband and children. Things have changed greatly in society since the end of the last century; the challenge will be to improve the living conditions of clergy families and hold onto their inspiration. And this is a challenge as much for us in the congregation as for the Church leaders.

Professor Phyllida Parsloe

Foreword

If you had asked me, five or ten years ago, to write an introduction to a book about the stress on clergy families I would have said, 'Stress? What stress?'

Yes, honestly.

If you'd pushed me, of course I could have instanced aspects of our lives which we experienced, because of my husband's calling, which the laity in our church didn't have. The night we moved in to our vicarage, for instance, nearly twenty years ago – a night of thick December snow, even in London – a woman rang our doorbell and said she had nowhere to sleep so could she move in... she and her children, as we obviously had plenty of room.

Not long afterwards, someone got us out of bed one Saturday morning, asking for the keys to the church. When I explained that we didn't have them and they were held by someone who lived in the next street, she exclaimed, horrified, 'But I couldn't disturb him at this hour of the morning! It's barely eight o'clock...' A little later, a member of the church with children the same age as ours, who was a trained counsellor, said she wished to volunteer her services. We responded enthusiastically, suggesting perhaps her name could be on the church noticeboard offering help, alongside Shaun (my husband)'s name and address. 'Certainly not!' she replied. 'It would be extremely dangerous, advertising where I live, with young children in the house...'

We laughed at such inconsistencies, and just got on with the job. Admittedly, until we acquired an answering machine, we never had time to bath our children, feed them or put them to bed: the hours between six and eight were just when everyone else was getting back from work and wanting to ring the vicar. And, until we learned to say, 'No cash, ever,' to callers at the door (though this didn't stop all of them), we had con men calling in an endless stream. We were disturbed at all hours of the day and night, robbed under our noses for years by a friend in the congregation, and people often strolled in and out of our house as if they owned it without bothering to ring the bell.

So our lives were different from those of the laity, it's true. But stress? The only thing that really stressed us, year on year, was the lack of money – but, despite this, we were very, very happy. Forgive the saccharine quip, but we didn't consider ourselves so much stressed as blessed. Shaun had a job he believed in and loved and one of eternal importance. Unlike our neighbours with families at a similar stage, he didn't have to leave the house at seven in the morning and come back after seven at night.

He read our children stories every bedtime (after we got the answerphone). He and I took our coffee breaks together, had lunch and tea together, and often worked in the same room, companionably, side by side. And we, the whole family, were all in it as a team. Our children prayed the Sunday School into being. They all joined the small music group I started, and eventually led it. They helped run the Harvest supper, looked after the elderly and entertained strangers. Their home was constantly being used for parties, wedding receptions, picnics – and, yes, sometimes rather noisy, musical prayer meetings, but never without their permission and presence. And, perhaps the greatest privilege of all, they often shared their supper with tramps, and made toasted sandwiches and sweet tea at midnight, and learned what it is that can reduce anyone to sleeping under Putney Bridge... They made friends their schoolmates would never have dreamed of, and saw an underside of England which others only read about in the papers. The result is that they can now get along with anyone: Bishop or bag-lady, Prime Minister or pauper.

We loved it. If you'd asked me about stress when we were living in an old-fashioned vicarage, being an old-fashioned clergy family, with an old-fashioned pastor-Bishop looking after us, I would have said, Come on. Don't be daft. Don't feel sorry for us. We are privileged. Our children have experiences none of their peers enjoy. We love it.

A few years ago, therefore, I would have found this book rather an alarming eye-opener. I might have thought, Perhaps the researchers saw what they set out to find. I would have recognised quite a lot of what they describe: the unspoken expectations and the irreconcilable demands, the unequal relationship between vicar and curate (and how easily it can be exploited). But I would have said, generally speaking, the Church of England muddles through somehow. It's not a bad way to live. Underpaid – and consequently, in a highly capitalist society, grossly under-valued and under-appreciated – but a lot of fun.

That was then. Since then I have seen things, witnessed comments, had experiences that I wouldn't have believed – that we didn't believe – possible. I have heard Christians say, of woefully inadequate housing, 'It's surely good enough for the clergy.' Or, from those whose incomes are ten times a vicar's stipend, 'It's not appropriate for those in ministry to earn more.' Or even, from someone whose house was worth over a million pounds, 'The congregation finds it inspiring when we see the clergy going without.'

I have heard of discrimination, injustice and abuse that would not be tolerated for five minutes in secular employment. I've seen bullying that would be reported, and promptly dealt with, in any other context of work. I have known clergy treated in a way that you wouldn't treat your dog.

So, sadly, nothing in this book surprises me now. Not only do I recommend it as strongly as I can, but I believe it to be essential reading for any who employ clergy, care about them and their families, have their welfare at heart or indeed have any contact with them at all. If you ever go to a church service, if only at Christmas and Easter; if you wish Anglicanism to outlast this generation in any recognisable form; if you have any interest at all in an ordained clergy being able to continue, then you must read this book. It contains objective research, expertly analysed, conducted according to recognised methods over several years. It makes for sombre reading.

By contrast, I can only give you my own personal, anecdotal explanations for the changes that have taken place. I can only tell you how we have found it; how our many clergy friends and their families have experienced and continue to experience it; and how my grandfather's life as a clergyman was so very different from what it would be now – fulfilling a high status, low stress role as he was then, which has become a low status, high stress one today.

Mine is a highly subjective response, and I realise many may disagree with me. But, unless you live with a member of the clergy or you are one yourself, dare I suggest you do so tentatively? For I'm sorry to say that my experience – our experience as a clergy family at the coal face – is that the changes over the last few decades to 'modernise' the church and bring it in line with secular society have been almost universally disastrous: certainly for the clergy themselves, and their wives (or husbands) and children; but also, though they may not realise this yet nor for some time to come, for the laity whom they attempt to serve. They have added to the stress of ministry to an almost unbearable degree. They have frequently made it difficult, sometimes almost impossible, to be effective. They have turned what was a wonderfully fulfilling and worthwhile vocation into what could accurately be described as a dead end and undoable job.

Perhaps there was an argument for overhauling it all. After all, no doctors that I know of still live at the surgery, and very few shopkeepers now live over the shop. But in that case it should have been done properly, in a businesslike way. If the Church had ruthlessly capitalised on church property at the right time, raised the bar rigorously for clergy admission, planned to employ a quarter as many for five times the salary in houses which they buy themselves and own, then it might still be a respectable profession attracting talented candidates. It would be very different, and I for one would be sad to see it go that way, but it would be justifiable and it might work well.

But the Church of England has not done this. As far as I can see, it has got rid of all the rather untidy and anachronistic aspects of clerical life which worked remarkably well, and replaced them with a poor, cheap, badly-run imitation of the secular world which doesn't work at all.

In every area, in my experience, this process of supposedly bringing the Church in line with modern life has added hugely to the stress of it, and indeed has often stopped clergy being clergy. Doing away with livings, and the introduction of compulsory retirement, for instance: time was when a clergyman had security, if not much money; and when it didn't matter so much that you didn't own your own house, because no one was going to take it away from you – at least not until you went to heaven when we all tend to lose it all anyway.

Multiple benefices, half stipends, house-for-duty (which, for the uninitiated, means you are not paid a bean)... all these make it impossible to fulfil a 'living'. How can you live out the life, if your pay only enables you to live half the time? How can you live in the community, if you are shared between six different communities? And how can you work part time, when the whole point of the clergy is to be, not to do? If someone rings your doorbell at three in the morning, distraught, are you supposed to stop and calculate whether it's still yesterday (which was one of your on-duty days for the parish) or today (which is an unpaid day) before you jump out of bed and open the door and put the kettle on, and try to persuade him that his life is worth living after all?

The most distressing change of all, in my view – because it is the most irreversible and has had the most devastating effect – has been the widespread selling off of arguably the Church's most precious material asset (perhaps even more than the church buildings themselves, which communities and heritage organisations might preserve if the Church could no longer afford to do so): her wonderful, versatile, priceless vicarages.

For it was our home, above all, which kept us going as a family when things were tough within the church – as, to be honest, they often were in the early years. Yes, even more than the support of other people, which is unpredictable after all. Having a spacious, solid, superbly well designed-for-the-purpose Victorian vicarage gave us a refuge which nothing else could have provided. And it was perfect for the job. It had, for instance, a porch for gentlemen of the road to shelter in when the weather was bitter, with a sturdy oak door that could be bolted to protect the family, but which had opaque, fortified glass in the top half so we could see whether our visitors were still there. It had a door in the bottom corner of the garden which led directly to the back of the church, so the congregation could spill out into the vicarage garden for coffee on sunny days. We had plenty of large rooms to accommodate the Sunday School; a kitchen big enough to feed twenty or more sitting down; a study which could comfortably accommodate as many and a drawing room just the same; and a room at the back of the house which couldn't be seen from the street so we could keep it as messy as we liked. It was a house built for the needs of ministry, and I've yet to see any modern clergy housing half so suitable.

Perhaps even more to the point, no matter what difficulties Shaun faced at work, no matter what strain this put on his family, no matter what other material deprivation they faced, he knew he was providing for his children a wonderful, hospitable home to invite their friends to, which more than compensated for never being able to afford holidays abroad or wear designer labels.

A year ago one of our children, after much sober reflection, told us he had decided to get ordained. After my initial shock, I found myself deeply thrilled: not only because it is always exciting when any young person discovers his future (the more so when that future is a selfless, idealistic vocation); but also because I found it such a vindication of his own upbringing. Yes, it has been full of love and laughter, and his decision said so.

But as the months have gone by since he made his announcement,

I confess I have found a chill settling on my heart. For years, Shaun has warned me that he is not confident there will be anything left in the clergy pensions pot by the time he is eligible and we need it (when we will also be needing to find our own home).

Now I find myself questioning whether there will be any stipends, any single benefices, any traditional vicarages, indeed anything to enable clergy to fulfil their livings at all in ten or twenty years' time. I long to support my son's decision, but it fills me with an awful dread. He had already come to his own conclusion that he could not study theology until he has worked to earn a living for some years: I have added the proviso that he must have a stake in his own property before he contemplates it, too. (And, I have thought but haven't said, probably a very high-earning wife...)

Recently, when I asked how many full time clergy there are in our diocese I was told, to my astonishment, that there is a shortage of young people with a vocation. My son believes he has just such a one. A generation ago, he would have gone straight to theological college from university, as his father did: young, energetic, and with his life's work ahead of him; confident that, whatever the other pressures, there would at least be a job for him after ordination, securely (if meagrely) paid employment for the rest of his working life, and decent housing for his children.

How could he do so today?

Anne Atkins

Authors' Note

Our experience in a broad range of professional and personal contexts has contributed, often in unexpected ways, to this study of clergy families.

Jean: Initially I worked as PA to a City director, a diplomat and the editor of the *Sunday Times*. I then joined the Chelmsford diocesan social work team where my brief included counselling clergy and their families. This showed the wide-ranging issues that clergy handle and the impact of the job on family life. Work consultancy to clergy and membership of bishops' committees for the care of clergy families in two dioceses for 20 years highlighted the hidden stresses faced by all family members.

After qualifying as a systemic family therapist, I joined the NHS in a Child and Adolescent Mental Health team. My private practice has specialized in issues of work/family stress and has included working with an employee assistance programme.

Chris: After National Service in The Black Watch, I became a Chartered Accountant in the City. Jean and I lived in East London at the Mayflower Family Centre and learned much about Christian work in urban areas from the vibrant thinking of those years. Following ordination, I served in three diverse parishes before becoming Team Rector of a large ecumenical parish in Harlow. Three years of family therapy training gave me new insights into work with families at the key stages of weddings, baptisms and funerals.

These experiences led to our PhD research at Bristol University. We carried out interviews with whole clergy families, parents and children together, so that the rewards and stresses of clergy family life could come into the public eye, and add a new dimension to previous studies of clergy and clergy couples. One group of six Church leaders, including three bishops, and another of counsellors to clergy families reflected with us on our findings after each of the three rounds of interviews. From these diverse perspectives we have been able to present a broad picture of dilemmas faced across the whole Church spectrum.

We hope our book will provide new insights for all ordained church leaders, as well as lay members such as churchwardens, church council members and others in key positions. Members and clergy of other churches feel our work resonates with their situation. Jewish friends and work colleagues have introduced us to their rabbis, suggesting that many of the issues have relevance for rabbis' families, and leaders in synagogues. Adult children of clergy families have expressed a keen interest throughout our work.

The issue of work/family stress currently has a high profile and many professionals, especially those involved in public roles such as personnel in the Armed Services, have questioned us closely about the general issues involved. We offer this book as a resource to them all.

PART ONE
Setting the Scene

1 Introduction

On a stormy night in 1859 a cliff face in Dorset crashed into the sea. There was no warning, no apparent sign of impending collapse, just a shattering tumble of boulders and a total change in the landscape. In April 2000 when part of Beachy Head collapsed, it was no surprise, as modern geologists saw tell-tale signs of the undermining of the rocks. The question was not if, but when.

Before we began the research on which this book is based, we had been aware over many years and from many sources that there was a long-term undermining of clergy and their families that needed to be addressed. We did not know the current extent of the difficulties.

A friend with long experience of marriage counselling was asked in the 1980s to lead a clergy wives' conference on marriage. The result was electric. 'The phone went on ringing for about three weeks afterwards', she told us, 'as first one then another of the clergy wives rang to talk'. She said it was obvious that some had held on to deep concerns and difficulties for years and it had taken real courage to talk to her. They were hesitant, tentative, almost as though they had no right to mention the issues or feared what might happen if these came to light. In 1990 a House of Bishops' marriage panel report highlighted a range of new concerns about clergy marriages.

There was certainly more publicity in both the church and secular press given to issues such as inappropriate behaviour from seemingly exemplary priests and the 'sudden' collapse of clergy marriages. For over 20 years, our work and membership of Bishop's committees in two dioceses for the care of clergy and their families showed that these were not simply one-off, newsworthy incidents but the tip of a larger iceberg.

The children could be caught up in the situation. Through our work we knew of serious problems they faced: a young teenager shop-lifting to keep in with a peer group on a tough estate, under-age pregnancy, drug addiction, serious bullying and much more. How far did the pressures of the job contribute to the difficulties? With new knowledge of stress, what were the issues that might prevent the underlying causes of these difficulties being addressed?

In the late 1980s and early 1990s several books were published, based on clergy themselves or clergy couples: *Clergy Stress: The Hidden Conflicts in Ministry*;[1] *Living with Stress: A Guide for Ministers and Church Leaders*;[2] *Clergy under Stress*;[3] and *Holy Matrimony? An exploration of Marriage and Ministry*.[4] All commented on the health effects of stress and the particular pressures and expectations of living life in the public eye. In 1996 'the inter-relationship of domestic and working lives in the armed forces' was examined in *Breaking Ranks*.[5]

No book, however, focused on whole families in any profession except in a clinical setting. We realized that our family therapy training and experience, outlined in the Preface, would allow us to conduct family interviews and bring an added perspective to all that was being said.

Many issues will overlap for the families of all clergy, men and women, including those of ordained couples, but some will be specific. We have considered general issues, and those for the families of male clergy, bearing in mind Marshall's[6] important statement that each piece of research looks at 'a unique and specific context'. We felt the specific issues for the families of women clergy and ordained couples, with different expectations and pressures, would need separate research. We hope that much that follows will also open new perspectives for the families of other professions as they explore their own unique and specific context.

1 Coate, M. A. (1989) *Clergy Stress The Hidden Conflicts in Ministry*. London: SPCK.
2 Horsman, S. (1989) *Living with Stress A Guide for Ministers and Church Leaders*. Cambridge: Lutterworth Press.
3 Fletcher, B. (1990) *Clergy under Stress*. London: Mowbray.
4 Kirk, M & Leary, T. (1994) *Holy Matrimony? An Exploration of Marriage and Ministry*. Oxford: Lynx.
5 Jessup, C. (1996) *Breaking Ranks Social Change in Military Communities*. London: Brassey's (UK) Ltd.
6 Marshall, C. (1985) Appropriate criteria for trustworthiness and goodness for qualitative research on education organisations, in *Quality and Quantity*, 19(4) 353–373.

II. THE OVERALL DILEMMA

We framed our overall dilemma as a question: '*Why does the church, one of whose tasks is to care for others, seem to find it so hard to care for its carers?*' This developed from our professional work with families in many settings and wide-ranging discussions with our senior family therapy consultant, Ros Draper.

We were seeking the whole family's perspective by talking to the children and parents together and this was essential to the process. We wanted to use an in-depth study rather than a widespread statistical one, so we recruited 20 clergy families from across the country. We also convened two Reference Groups whose purpose was to comment on what the families said and to give us further information about the Church as an organization. The Groups each had six members. One was made up of people involved in the pastoral care and counselling of clergy and their families; the other of those in positions of leadership in the Church, including three bishops.

We thought it was important not only to take a snapshot of the families' and Groups' responses but also to see how their perspectives and responses might change over a period of time. All the family interviews and Group meetings were therefore completed three times at annual intervals. This broad base would give us a more rounded picture of the situation at different levels of the Church. It would also help us to understand how the levels related to one another, and to assess the issues of the overall dilemma above.

Confidentiality was of prime importance and was emphasized to everyone involved. Details have been changed to prevent identification for those who might be tempted to play 'spot the family'. There is always the possibility that we will have changed the details in such a way that they are similar to those of a different family, as many comparable events and issues occur for clergy families generally. If the information appears to fit a family known to readers, their detective work is almost certainly mistaken!

III. THE FAMILY ISSUES

As an introduction we look briefly at several issues that throw light on what generally helps families to cope, and why they might be struggling in a particular way at a particular time.

One of the most important considerations is the context in which a family is set. This includes not only their accommodation but also friendship and support networks within the community and from their extended families, especially at times of change. We also explore the causes of stress, and how stress can develop and accumulate for a family as well as an individual. We look at how life-cycle changes may cause stress in families and organizations, and sometimes in both at the same time. When difficulties coincide in more than one of these areas, they can cause more serious problems.

These are key issues for all families and are based on ideas and theories developed in the whole systemic family therapy field. We use them throughout our work, both in planning the interviews and assessing all that the families and Reference Groups said. Several other frameworks that can give a wider perspective on clergy families are threaded through the book. One of the most significant has been the 'Double Bind', outlined in Chapter 11.

For clarity we have divided the book into six short Parts. In this introductory Part we outline the structures of the Church of England and the Support Systems provided for clergy and their families as this is the context within which they live and work.

Part II sets the wider scene. We think briefly about how previous research on clergy and other professional groups can help us in our work. In particular we consider issues for those in the public eye, such as the police, local councillors and the armed forces. We also look at stress models, and outline how the research was set up and carried out.

Part III covers the Curacy Stage explored in the first interviews, and the issues raised by the families and Reference Groups at this initial point in their journey.

Part IV is a 'Pause for Thought' as we examine ideas that can help to throw light on the whole experience of clergy families.

Part V covers the issues from the second and third interviews discussed by the families, and the perspective of the Reference Groups on the families' ongoing situation.

In Part VI we consider the wider response of the Reference Groups, and reflect on the Dilemmas faced by the leadership, counsellors and lay church leaders as well as the families. Finally we review the implications of the research, and set out recommendations based on all the information we received, as well as on practical and theoretical ideas explored at each stage.

Our aim is to see how the whole system of the Church fits together and how the different levels and aspects of such a complex organization interlock and support one another. Within this wider context, we hope the book will bring new perspectives and understanding to all involved with clergy families, especially churchwardens and other local leaders, as well as to the families themselves and the wider leadership.

The cliff face in 1859 collapsed without warning. The undermining of clergy families may equally be hidden. Throughout the book we shall highlight issues that strengthen the families of clergy or may threaten their stability. Dilemmas within the whole Church system that cause important family issues to be overlooked should also come into focus.

On a broader level, the Church as a whole is involved in the lives of many other families at key life stages through baptisms, weddings and funerals. If we bear these issues in mind, they may bring new perspectives in our contact with the wider public.

2 The Structures of the Church of England

I. CHURCH STRUCTURES

We saw in Chapter 1 that the overall situation in which families are set plays an important part in how they cope with change and challenge in all parts of their family life. For clergy families, the inherited structures of the Church of England are a significant part of that context, so we shall consider briefly how the structures have emerged over several centuries. These have frequently reflected not only spiritual insights, but also social and political attitudes of a particular stage in history. The result has been that a very diverse and complex·system now surrounds clergy families.

The document, *Order in Diversity*,[1] gives helpful information on Church systems and sheds some light on how contradictions and anomalies may have arisen within the Church. We shall touch on key issues that have a particular impact on the families.

1. The task of ministry and the parish system

When Henry VIII declared himself Supreme Head of the Church in England in place of the Pope, the Church became the official or Established Church under his authority. Since that time, the Monarch, the State and the Church have been entwined and the significance of this will come to light as the story unfolds.

Order in Diversity shows that the Church has a very wide remit. Its purpose is 'to proclaim the gospel in worship, word, sacrament and service and to provide pastoral care and access to public worship for every person and every community in the land'. It has 'accepted that it

---

1 Advisory Board of Ministry (1993) *Order in Diversity: Variety, Numbers and Issues for the Ordained Ministry of the Church of England.* London: ABM Publications.

has a responsibility towards every aspect of the nation's life. Throughout the country every acre is included within parish boundaries, confirming that the Church accepts a care for all that takes place within the land' – an interesting comment on the idea that religion and politics do not mix.

The parish system is at the heart of the Church. Parish boundaries have been redrawn as populations have moved, and some parishes have been amalgamated with others. Over time parishes have been grouped into 42 dioceses across the country. Each has its own bishop as its spiritual leader who has one or more assistant or suffragan bishops. Each diocese is also divided into archdeaconries, between two and six according to population and area, with an archdeacon forming a further level of leadership under the bishops.

The purpose of the Church, as pointed out in *Order in Diversity*, is not only to be fulfilled by clergy, as 'all Christians, ordained and lay, are called to full-time ministry of the gospel'. This is, of course, emphasized throughout the New Testament.[2] 'However, in order to serve the needs of the Church a number of people have been called and ordained to serve God full-time within Church structures'. An additional point is that 'the way this ministry is exercised has changed radically in the past three decades and this change will continue . . . in the new millennium'.

A large number of clergy retired in the 1990s and fewer are now being ordained. We shall note the families' and Groups' impression of lay members' involvement and *their* call to 'full-time ministry'. In *Ministry Issues for the Church of England*,[3] Gordon Kuhrt emphasizes the increasing part lay members will play in ministry in the future, with the smaller number of clergy focussing more on a teaching and training role.

2. The patronage system

Henry VIII also 'dissolved' the monasteries and much Church land was confiscated, becoming the property of the Crown, or of those in the King's favour. One result was that new lay owners then became

---

2 For example Paul's letter to the Philippians ch. 1, v. 5, and Peter's First Letter ch. 2, v. 9.

3 Kuhrt, G. (2001) *Ministry Issues for the Church of England*. London: Church House Publishing.

patrons of the parishes within their boundaries. This gave them the right to appoint clergy there and also to receive the income from this former church land. They paid clergy at their discretion, so there were huge discrepancies in clergy pay. For example the owner's annual income was £800 at Hornchurch in Essex; the vicar's was £55. Many clergy had much less and curates had a bare minimum.

As a result of these changes, nearly half of all clergy appointments were no longer under bishops' control,[4] and patrons often appointed their younger sons to their local parish. In the past 50 years lay patrons have gradually returned to the bishops their right to appoint clergy or have worked in consultation with them, but patronage has often limited the planning and control of bishops and other church leaders.

3. The freehold and appointments

Until 2004, clergy were granted the freehold of the parish when they were appointed, and their freehold continued while they held that particular post. Historically this was to protect them from being driven out by local lobbying or being dismissed unfairly because of vested interest. The freehold, however, meant that clergy could remain in that parish as long as they wished and led to a great sense of independence for many clergy.

Bishops then had less freedom to deploy clergy or even to dismiss them for unsatisfactory performance, although they could withdraw their licence for sexual or financial 'misdemeanour'. The Disciplinary Measure of 2003 now lays down more precise criteria for performance and behaviour. If these are not met, clergy are given two official warnings by the archdeacon, followed by an independent disciplinary hearing if performance does not improve.

The lack of flexibility over appointments, resulting from the freehold, appears as a problem in *Order in Diversity*, as do family issues. 'The expectation that family considerations, including children's education and spouse's career, should be given full weight is now a powerful limitation to the deployability of clergy, making it more difficult than it might otherwise be ... For some who have the pastoral care of clergy and the responsibility to ensure that parishes are

---

4 Morgan, K. O. (ed.) (1984) *The Oxford Illustrated History of Britain*. London: Guild Publishing.

served by suitable clergy, it can be depressing and frustrating to find that other factors are acquiring a higher value.' We shall note the type of 'other factors' involved in families' decisions about appointments and their importance for the family. Letters to the *Church Times* about clergy deployment (Chapter 12 I .1) are particularly interesting in giving perspectives from both sides.

Under the Terms and Conditions of Service Legislation of 2004 the freehold was replaced by fixed terms for all new appointments, but those who already had a freehold are able to remain in their parish until retirement, normally at 70 if they wish.

4.   A stipend and tied housing

Clergy are 'required to be resident within the parish where they serve'. *Order in Diversity* also says that in order to sustain the ordained ministry the Church has made available a 'stipend, which is intended to be sufficient to meet the reasonable needs of the clergy and their dependants'. Clergy now have an income level set by their diocese but with reference to national guidelines. The level of their working expenses and other allowances may still be significantly different from parish to parish.

The Church has also 'provided accommodation so that clergy may live in the parish without disadvantage'. Even comparatively young children may be concerned about this tied housing. One question we asked in the third interview was, 'What would have to happen for your father to look for a new job outside the ministry?' In one family, after other members had given their ideas, the father said he would find it very hard to continue in ministry if his wife died or if he had a serious or terminal illness. Immediately the daughter, a particularly bright, open 12-year-old said, 'It would be better if Mummy died because then we'd still have a house to live in'. The whole family laughed and she shrugged and laughed too. 'Oh, you know what I mean!' It was obvious that they did, and there was no embarrassment, but the poignancy of her anxiety about the future was not lost.

5.   The tithe

Historically a small area of land, the Glebe, was set aside to make extra practical provision for clergy, and tenants of this land gave a tithe, or 10 per cent of their harvest to the priest. 'In return clergy maintained the chancel of the church and saw to the provision of church worship'.[5] The increase in the value of land during the eighteenth century led to two significant changes for clergy. The tithe was gradually replaced by rent and as land values rose following the Enclosure Movement, rent increased and so did clergy wealth. Clergy gain meant a loss of income for parishioners and caused considerable resentment. Patrons' wealth increased even more and many built larger, more imposing houses for clergy, which identified them with the landed gentry.

Even after the agricultural depression of the 1880s and the sharp fall in income from the Glebe, the high status housing continued to give an image of the former affluent lifestyle of many clergy for nearly a century more, and a sense of separation from the majority of parishioners.

6. Isolation

The families and the Groups often mentioned isolation, a theme which was explored by Collins in 1996 in *Jane Austen and the Clergy*.[6] He points out that in the eighteenth and nineteenth centuries the clergy would have trained in the stimulating atmosphere of Oxford or Cambridge. Once they were ordained, they could find themselves isolated in a country village, with no literate parishioners apart from the squire. Russell[7] points out, 'In the Victorian age characterized by activity, achievement, success, and almost boundless opportunity for the energetic and determined, there was increasing concern for the loneliness and stagnation of clergy ministering in small country parishes.'

The position of vicarages may add to this isolation today. A significant proportion of our research families lived in houses built in the last 40 years, beside the church or within the church complex, especially in city areas. They spoke of the resulting isolation from the community. Many recent replacements for historic vicarages have been based as much on practical and financial considerations for the Church as on the needs of clergy families. We shall consider issues of physical, social and mental isolation for current clergy families in all their different situations.

---

5 Hey, D. (ed.) (1996) Oxford Companion to Local and Family History. Oxford: Oxford University Press.
6 Collins, I. (1994) *Jane Austen and the Clergy*. London: Hambledon Press.
7 Russell, A. (1984) *The Clerical Profession*. London: SPCK.

7. A lasting image and the clergy role

The historic image was not only set in stone through housing, but was also captured in much well-known contemporary literature. Both these issues have had a lasting impact on the public's impression of the clergy. In his *Rural Rides* Cobbett[8] speaks of the unprintable language about clergy which he was hearing on all sides, often linked to the tithe, as he criss-crossed the country in the 1820s. The change between two of George Eliot's novels in particular reflects the sharp change in image at this time. *Scenes from Clerical Life*[9] has moving stories of dedicated, financially insecure clergy. Later, she describes the priest in *Middlemarch*,[10] Edward Casaubon, as 'a man of wealth enough to give lustre to his piety'. This is just one of many portrayals of inept, unattractive figures unable to relate to their peers or their parishioners. Elizabeth Bennett describes her ordained cousin in *Pride and Prejudice*[11] as a conceited, pompous, narrow-minded, silly man. Recent films of nineteenth-century classics have served to reinforce these confused or distorted images.

At the end of the nineteenth century, attitudes to the clergy are shown in a letter from Lord Chesterfield to a squire about choosing suitable professions for his sons. 'I recommend the Army or Navy to a boy of warm constitution, strong animal spirits and a cold genius; to one of quick, lively and distinguished parts – the law; to a good, dull and decent boy, the Church'.[12] The image and the ambivalence live on.

Why does this matter now? G. V. Bennett[13] highlights why eighteenth- and nineteenth-century literature and drawings throw light on both the clergy image and the clergy role today. He points out that the largest collection of Prints and Drawings in the British Library is that devoted to the clergy of the Church of England. Apart from official portraits, most of the drawings are caricatures.

As he says, 'the ridiculous is always more memorable than the serious' and much of the work is social comment but 'there is virtually

---

8   Cobbett, W. (1973) *Rural Rides 1821–32*. London: Dent.
9   Eliot, G. (1985) *Scenes of Clerical Life*, (1st edn 1858). London: Penguin Classics.
10 Eliot, G. (1985) *Middlemarch*, (1st edn 1871). London: Penguin Classics.
11 Austen, J. (1985) *Pride and Prejudice*. London: Penguin Classics .
12 Bradshaw, J. (1892) *The Letters of Philip Dormer Stanhope, Earl of Chesterfield*. London: Allen & Unwin.
13 Bennett, G.V. (1988) *To the Church of England*. London: Churchman.

nothing showing an ordinary parish priest doing his ordinary pastoral work'. Significantly, he 'suspects the real reason is that the English have always been uncertain about a clergyman's role in society, and they have taken refuge in caricature to hide a certain unease'.

Parishioners today may have little idea about the wider role of clergy, apart from services, weddings and funerals. On the other hand, they may have their own specific ideas about how that role should be carried out, leading to expectations, however unrealistic, from different groups at different times.

'Expectations' was a key theme throughout the research, and extended to all family members. Such expectations are not new. Russell[14] suggests that professional roles in Victorian times were connected with status rather than with tasks. All professionals were expected to conform to a particular life-style, with an emphasis on duty and service. This included the 'ancient notion that the professional man is never off duty, blurring the boundaries between work and leisure'.

Today clear boundaries such as surgery times, office hours and alternate shifts allow most professionals to be off duty at specific times. Clergy, however, are still assumed by the general public, and by many members of their own congregations, to be constantly available. Their home is also seen as a place of work, so demands at any hour may come into the home.

8.   Reflections

We have looked at the inherited structures of the Church to see how these influence the setting for clergy family life. The priest is required to live in the house provided, so this dictates many aspects of the family's home life for the whole period of any appointment. If the house is easily identified this will link the family immediately with the Church. We shall see from all that the families say what impact this has on other people's perception of them as a family and as individuals, and how this influences their friendships and support. We shall monitor any 'unease' that is shown because either the public or church members are uncertain about what the clergy role involves, and the way this may lead to particular expectations. How far do the

---

14 See n. 7 above.

unclear boundaries that are part of these uncertainties lead to intrusion into the home and family life?

In future, posts will be time limited. Concerns that the family may have at the end of a contract because they are in tied housing will be noted.

The State still has an influence over senior appointments and over some sections of the Church's finance. The leadership's sense of control in making decisions may be limited by this involvement as well as by some remaining aspects of the Patronage system. All these issues will be part of our overall assessment of the impact of the Church's structures on clergy families.

3 Professional Support Systems

In Chapter 2 we saw that by living in the vicarage, the families of clergy become closely identified with the parish and tasks of ministry. The dioceses provide various systems to help clergy in their task and to support clergy family members. We shall see how these underpin the stability of the families, and note any uncertainties about the systems that may cause the families stress or concern.

I.   FINANCIAL SUPPORT

1.   Stipend and housing

Funding for clergy pay and housing comes from three main sources: direct giving by church members or the public, fees from weddings and funerals, and income from accumulated investments.

These 'accumulated investments' stem from the ancient endowments of the Church and a fund called Queen Anne's Bounty, set up in 1704 for the relief of ill-housed and poor clergy. In 1948 these were amalgamated and the Church Commissioners were established with responsibility for the combined funds. Although the Commissioners regularly submit themselves to scrutiny by the General Synod, the State still appoints the First Church Estates Commissioner, and the Second Church Commissioner is an MP who answers questions in Parliament on Church matters. Therefore, this is an area where Church and State are still intertwined..

In 1993 a Church Commissioners' management decision on investment led to a substantial loss of the capital value of the invested funds. As a result investment income fell sharply. Since that time the Commissioners have greatly reduced grants to dioceses to cover stipends and pensions. Most future funding for these will have to be found from direct giving. The majority of the Commissioners' investment income is now used to cover pension commitments up to 1998. This has put considerable financial pressure on parishes. It has also changed the balance between clergy and lay members who now directly contribute the majority of the money to pay the clergy. The idea that clergy should be paid a stipend and housed independently without pressure from local interests may now change. The situation is sufficiently recent that its full impact may take time to emerge.

These factors have created uncertainty about the adequacy of future financial support for clergy and their families while clergy are in post, and considerable concern about pension support once they retire. This is linked again to tied housing. The provision of the house is part of the 'package' that clergy receive but, unlike other professionals, they are of course unable to invest that part of their 'income' in a mortgage to secure a home for the future. The uncertainty about future financial provision is therefore particularly significant.

2. Terms and conditions

Order in Diversity[1] points out that 'in the Church of England, housing, stipend and pension entitlement are still consequent upon institution or licence to a particular position or office. There has never been any acceptance ... that those who are ordained will necessarily be supported by the Church'. A proposal in 1967[2] that clergy should be taken 'onto the strength' of a diocese, as in the Methodist Church, was not accepted. Few jobs are secure in our fast changing world, but few also involve tied housing.

---

1 Advisory Board of Ministry (1993) *Order in Diversity: Variety, Numbers and Issues for the Ordained Ministry of the Church of England.* London: ABM Publications.
2 Morley, W. F. (Chairman) (1967) *Partners in Ministry: Being the Report of the Commission on the Deployment and Payment of the Clergy.* London: Church Information Office.

II. PROFESSIONAL AND SPIRITUAL SUPPORT AND PASTORAL CARE

1. Ongoing training and review

In the majority of professions today there is a requirement for ongoing professional development. For newly ordained priests, three years of post-ordination training are provided in their dioceses. After that time, continuing Ministerial Education (CME) grants are made available to individual clergy to help pay for relevant ongoing training. The grant varies from diocese to diocese according to policy and resources.

Clergy are answerable to their bishop. Episcopal reviews are held annually in most dioceses and are usually compulsory. These have been described as 'a process by which the Bishop, or the Archdeacon as his representative, meets with an individual minister in his Area to review the current state of his or her ministry and its future development and to relate it to the diocesan strategy for ministry'.[3] This suggests a move from a more individually focused ministry to one positioned within the overall strategy of the diocese. The review may be carried out alternately with the Archdeacon, so a review with the Bishop may happen once in two years.

2. Deanery support

As well as a diocese being divided into two or more archdeaconries, these in turn are divided into deaneries, each with several parishes within a local area. The clergy meet regularly each month at deanery meetings for worship and discussion, sometimes with a speaker. The bishop consults local clergy and then appoints one of them as rural/ area dean for a fixed term to act as a support to clergy and a channel of general communication between them and the leadership. As this is not an external appointment, their seniority and positioning within the structure varies greatly from deanery to deanery and so does the actual support they give to clergy. Rural/area deans of course also have their own parish to run.

3. Spiritual support

Clergy can refer themselves to trained spiritual directors for guidance

---

3 Letter sent to clergy in the Chelmsford Diocese by the Bishop (1996).

and ongoing spiritual development. Retreats are available to clergy but both these and counselling sessions may have to be funded from their annual training allocation. If a series of counselling sessions should be necessary this might use up all of a 'training grant' for the year. Retreats may also be provided for clergy spouses.

4. Pastoral care

Pastoral care and counselling are organized by individual dioceses, which may appoint a pastoral care director, a team of qualified counsellors, and/or a confidential help-line. These may also be available to clergy families. For clergy spouses, dioceses may organize conferences, and deaneries may have support or discussion groups. Some dioceses provide counselling across diocesan boundaries to aid confidentiality. Other agencies may be used such as the Westminster Pastoral Foundation, which set up a Clergy Marriage Consultation Service in 1989. Some funding for counselling may be available from a Bishop's discretionary fund.

III REFLECTIONS ON THE STRUCTURES OF THE CHURCH AND SUPPORT SYSTEMS

The variation in systems throughout the Church is striking. The complexity of the historical factors behind Church structures means uniform systems or procedures cannot be taken for granted. Parishes and dioceses vary greatly in size, tradition and available finance. The appointment systems, stipends and expenses have been equally variable and the independence of the freehold has added to uncertainty about the clergy role.

Bishops and other Church leaders have to find a path through the complexities of the system. The way problems have been solved within the Church historically, by the State, the monarch and the Church, has frequently sent strong conflicting messages about faith and spiritual values throughout the church network and to the public. What the Church has said and what it has done have not necessarily been the same.[4]

---

4   Schein, E. (1985) *Organizational Culture and Leadership*. San Francisco: Jossey-Bass.

Different sections of society have then been alienated from the Church as changes have seemed to favour one group or another. As Russell suggests, this has often resulted in a clergy/laity divide. If 'all Christians, ordained and lay, are called to full-time ministry of the gospel', it is important that divisions between clergy and laity should not make it harder to work together.

Recent changes in Church Commissioners' grants have put great financial pressure on the stipends and housing funds of dioceses and this pressure will continue. Pensions will depend on public giving being maintained and increased.

Training and professional support structures for clergy again vary considerably from area to area and only post-ordination training is compulsory. Continuing Ministerial Education grants are available but are limited and may be needed to pay for spiritual direction or counselling. This suggests unclear boundaries between the distinct and separate nature of professional, spiritual, and pastoral provision.

This brief outline suggests that there are issues causing stress and the undermining of clergy families, which need to be clarified and addressed. The information from the families and the Reference Groups may help us to judge the seriousness of the issues.

PART TWO
Background, Methodology and Family Stress

4 Background Perspectives

I. WIDER PERSPECTIVES ON PROFESSIONAL STRESS

The issues explored in Part I suggested that the Church system surrounding clergy families is complex and sometimes contradictory. The whole family is also in the public eye with all the expectations this may bring. Anyone holding a public position has particular pressures on them and we wanted to consider the similarities and differences for clergy and their families. We looked at previous studies on clergy as well as research on other jobs relating to the wider public. These highlighted common themes and issues for us to follow up with the whole family in mind.

1. Clergy and clergy families

In her book on clergy stress, based on her counselling experience, psychologist MaryAnn Coate[1] emphasizes 'sources of stress for ministers that are not shared by other caring professionals'. These are 'likely to be permanent and insidious until they force themselves on our attention in threatening and potentially destructive ways'. She suggests that the likely effects of these hidden conflicts in ministry would be illness, alcohol or other drug dependence, and emotional or marital breakdown.

She compares ministers with those in comparable positions of community leadership, and considers that 'those in ministry do not cope very well with this sort of pressure'. She is drawing on those referred for counselling so we shall need to assess her statement in a wider context, such as the demands and supports in each setting. However, it raises the question of whether aptitude as well as training,

---

1   Coate, M. A. (1989) *Clergy Stress: The Hidden Conflicts in Ministry.* London: SPCK.

to cope with the specific pressures and conflicts for ministers, is addressed during selection and training, and by the leadership in their ongoing management roles.

Dr. Horsman[2] also explores the risks to health from the 'many inherent stresses for clergy, some shared with other jobs, others specific to it'. In her guide for ministers and church leaders, *Living with Stress*, she emphasizes 'the importance of *seeking* help for stress' to prevent these health risks. She comments that 'most churches want their minister to be a married bachelor, married to relate better to those with family problems, and single to have endless time and energy for helping others without being tied down to the demands of domestic pressures'.

Dr. Horsman administers the Society of Mary and Martha. This offers widespread support and care for clergy and clergy families, through counselling, ministerial review, residential holidays and a national help-line. In 2002 the Society consulted widely and produced *Affirmation and Accountability*,[3] as a 'toolbox for action within the whole church system'. It addresses both small and larger changes needed to bring a wider cultural change in the church, and suggests that in this two-way bargain 'the problem belongs to us all. The church cannot afford not to take better care of its clergy'.

An issue explored by Fletcher[4] in *Clergy under Stress* is the importance of balance in a job between demands, job supports and constraints, and the strains that result when the balance is wrong. He suggests that 'high demands in the right circumstances can provide stimulation and utilize abilities; under-utilization and boredom are among the most potent stressors and usually occur in work environments where supports are low and constraints high'. This balance for the clergy will be part of our assessment.

Like Horsman, Kirk and Leary[5] suggest that church members expect clergy couples to be role models of the ideal domestic relationship but also totally available for people's needs. In *Holy Matrimony* they comment on the 'paucity of professional recognition'.

---

2   Horsman, S. (1989)) *Living with Stress: A Guide for Ministers and Church Leaders*. Cambridge: Lutterworth Press..

3   Lee, C. and Horsman, S. (2002) *Affirmation and Accountability*. Exeter: The Society of Mary and Martha.

4   Fletcher, B (1990) *Clergy under Stress*. London: Mowbray.

5   Kirk, M. & Leary, T. (1994) *Holy Matrimony An exploration of marriage and ministry*. Oxford: Lynx.

They found 'significant levels of illness or psychological trouble by any standards' and a high incidence of depression in wives. They point out that 'it is the non-ordained partner who will usually show signs of stress first, if pressures on the marriage and family are not successfully coped with'.

They recommend new criteria for selection and training including psychological testing, and a career structure with possible time out of parochial ministry to increase stimulation, as there are so few senior posts. They also suggest that the policy of tied housing should be re-examined, as owning their own house would provide 'a boundary between the private and the public, and one source of depression, especially in wives would disappear'. This extends Horsman's comment that 'by living in tied accommodation ministers forfeit a highly valued security in our home-owning society, pay the price when they retire, and their children forfeit property inheritance'.

2. Families of public figures

In order to check Coate's statement that 'clergy do not cope very well with the stresses' they face, compared with other community leaders, we looked at research on public figures. Several common themes were highlighted where a parent's position meant the family was in the public eye.

Janet Finch[6] shows how work-related structures may limit a partner's choices. For example doctors, clergy, the police and MPs are required to be 'set apart' because they have access to privileged information, and do a job where members of the public must be treated on an equal footing. She suggests that the risks of breaching confidentiality and of favouritism are 'greatly enhanced if the work is conducted in a settled and identifiable community'.

Finch also raises the issue of spouses 'experiencing some of the consequences of being a public figure without having been appointed, elected or paid. They will be expected to behave as if they had been, and they and their families will be under scrutiny. Two consequences for social relationships are the feeling of being kept at arm's length by other people, and the recognition that it is inappropriate to have close friends in the community.'

6   Finch, J. (1983) *Married to the Job*. London: George Allen & Unwin.

'The constitution of the home as a semi-public place through its use as a work base is certainly experienced as an intrusion, and the distinction between work and non-work becomes blurred in terms of both space and activities.' Finch assesses the competition between work and family time. She suggests that for clergy available at home, 'the situation is structured so that any performance of domestic tasks appears to be an alternative to work'.

3. Local Authority elected councillors and their families

Local Authority elected councillors[7] find setting personal/professional boundaries difficult, particularly where social and leisure activities are tied up with political activities. They are often identified and approached by members of the public with problems or requests both on and off duty. Sometimes they are abused in person or in the press. At times family members face expectations of involvement, and of particular attitudes or behaviour, and children may be criticised by teachers or others because of their parents' identity.

Some said that friends and acquaintances tend to see them differently once they are councillors and are wary of them, which parallels Finch's comment that 'being a public figure essentially means being defined in terms of work for the purposes of almost all social contacts'.

For most councillors, in contrast to clergy, extra hours are separate from their paid employment, not a continuation of their normal work into 'leisure' time. The job can also be short-term with councillors not standing for re-election because the workload and demands are too heavy, or if they reach a new stage of family life.

4. The police

Two interesting issues relevant to clergy stress are raised in a paper on Occupational Trauma in British Police Officers.[8] This suggests that

---

7 Barron, J., Crawley, G., and Wood, T. (1987) *Married to the Council? The Private Costs of Public Service*, Report to the Leverhulme Trust. Bristol: Bristol Polytechnic.

8 Mitchell-Gibbs, J. and Mitchell, S. A. (1996) *Occupational Trauma in British Police Officers*, Paper presented at the First European Conference on Traumatic Stress in Emergency Services, Peacekeeping Operations and Humanitarian Aid Organisations, Sheffield, UK, 17–20 March.

the failure to express traumatic experiences may result in poorer psychological and physical health. Displaying signs of stress may be considered personal and professional weakness, may damage career advancement and be in conflict with police culture. If these experiences are not expressed, they could reduce the potential for support as well as influencing coping behaviours.

A second issue is that repeated stressful experiences may accumulate and lead to psychological disorders. One event, frequently experienced and perceived as distressing even for long serving officers, is attending the scene of sudden death. Peer-group counselling and critical incident debriefings are used in British police forces as appropriate interventions, on the basis that police officers share a strong sense of group identity, solidarity and acknowledged segregation from other social groups.

5. The armed services

Several points in two books on the armed services by Ruth Jolly[9] and Chris Jessup[10] relate to issues for clergy families. They suggest that a younger generation of service personnel are not less committed to the Military but more committed to involvement in family life, and may be uncertain where to call the dividing line. Jolly says that 'most conflicts are concerned with divided loyalties between the family and military responsibilities'.

'When there are difficulties, senior officers who have overcome specific problems themselves, may believe that their own solutions are the right answer for anyone else in a similar situation. When facing stress, personnel may therefore not feel the essential requirements have been met: that they have been heard and understood, and that they have options which help them to stay in control of the situation. The possibility of independence and self-determination are firmly linked to the organization's response. Helplessness remains for them and their families while old patterns and assumptions remain unchallenged.'

More military families now own their own house, otherwise they

---

9 Jolly, R. (1987) *Mitary Man, Family Man: Crown Property?* London: Brassey's Defence Publishers.
10 Jessup, C. (1996) *Breaking Ranks: Social Change in Military Communities.* London: Brassey's (UK) Ltd.

'cannot decide on the proportion of their income they will spend on housing, and without security (of a house) comes lack of choice'. With the demands placed on the family, Jolly concludes that 'it is probably true to say that families that can withstand the pressures of military life are very strong units indeed'. We shall note the strengths of clergy families in the wide variety of situations they face.

II.   EXPLORING ISSUES FOR CLERGY FAMILIES IN THE UNITED STATES

We spent five weeks looking at issues for clergy and their families in the United States. We interviewed an American Episcopal family with three children, using the same structure we had used with our 20 families. Issues were very similar to those for the families in the UK except that, like most US clergy, they owned their own house, which was a significant difference. They spoke of the difficulty of making independent decisions because of restrictions of the system, and the sense of isolation.

However, the two American bishops we met, one appointed within the previous two years, one approaching retirement, both echoed the need for a 'fresh vision of ministry that doesn't perpetuate inappropriate dependence in clergy'.[11] The bishops spoke of the confusion they faced between providing support for clergy within a management framework – as in any management situation – and counselling them.

We also explored two major research projects, set up after widespread discussions by the Episcopal Church, to see if issues for the church in America were relevant to our own work. Both these projects suggested that despite 'significant attempts to strengthen clergy leadership and to support their work', clergy families were in trouble and the church had been slow to develop resources to serve them.

The Cornerstone Project[12] had four areas of enquiry: the role of bishops in relation to clergy; the ideal (or healthy) clergy person; the

---

11 Episcopal Church Foundation and The Alban Institute (1989) *The Cornerstone Project: Personal and Professional Development of the Clergy of the Episcopal Church*. New York: The Episcopal Church Foundation.

12 See n. 11 above.

current state of the clergy; and bridging the gap between the current state and the ideal. The Project report highlighted several issues relating to our research: the isolation of clergy from bishops; a sense of competition between clergy because of infrequent contact and a lack of benchmarks by which to measure progress; and confusion over the current clergy role.

The Project report also suggested that within the Episcopal Church there is no theology of the married priesthood, a central issue for our work. It urges 'our best theological minds to tackle this issue and put to rest the ambivalence and struggle with which so many have lived for so long. There is no theological reason to assert that either marriage or ordination is more sacred than the other'. There was a need for 'a sound theological basis for the integration of these dual sacraments and vows'.

A referral group from all the bodies responsible for Episcopal clergy in the USA felt the findings showed a need for honesty rather than denial about the present situation. As well as a new look at the bishops' role there should be the 'fresh vision of ministry that doesn't perpetuate inappropriate dependence in clergy' mentioned above. The referral group also felt that the context of ministry was noticeably absent and very little had been said about the minister's family, both issues at the heart of our own research. The report also said that if the emphasis were on individual change it would not bring about the 'sea change' that was necessary to revitalize the church and its priesthood.

The Episcopal Families Network research[13] asked clergy couples to choose eight out of 22 items that were important for their health and well-being, in order to establish a health index. The items chosen were:

- A sense of accomplishment in their ministry
- Satisfaction from their work in the Church
- Not thinking seriously about leaving parish ministry
- A feeling of growing in spiritual depth
- Being successful in overcoming difficulties
- Having supportive relations in the parish so they did not feel lonely or isolated

---

13 Episcopal Families Network (1988) *Episcopal Clergy Families in the 80s.* New York: The Episcopal Church Foundation.

- The congregation understanding their needs for private time
- The families feeling they had 'enough money to live on comfortably' which linked to both the priest's satisfaction in his job and the health index score.

Recognizing that 'stress in one member leads to stress in others' the research asked if any family member was suffering from any of 13 listed problems, They had expected that the most serious problems would occur in a small proportion of the families with several problems in the same family. They found that 'no less then 60% of clergy couples had at least one serious problem in the immediate family although some families with other positive factors were still moderately healthy on the index'.

Statistics from other diocesan sources suggested that, despite confidentiality, there was under-reporting of serious problems, so researchers were left with the question 'What is the whole truth?'

III. CLERGY CHILDREN

Three clergy children who wrote of their experiences graphically illustrate some of these issues. In Coasting[14] the lone sailor, Jonathan Raban, paints a picture of how, having 'sailed two thousand miles to reach the Isle of Man', he had, metaphorically, 'arrived at the place where the voyage really began – this insular, enclosed world'. 'The Island was Home ... the home I'd always been running away from. The parsonage was our island. The house was surrounded by a high wild hedge which rolled and broke like the sea. The invisible world beyond this hedge kept on changing: one year there was a pallid brick council estate on the fringe of a city; the next a Hampshire village with rustic thatch and a Common of gorse and primroses, where adders sinisterly coiled in the grass.'

Visitors came from that outside world, 'as if they'd made a sea crossing to reach us ... looking formal, shy and ill at ease'. He learned to live a double life, adjusting to both the houses on the estate, and the middle-class homes on the further rim of the village. And there was a third life too, as he mingled on the sly with the 'come over kids', and

---

14 See n. 8 above.

expressed, with them, scorn at his father and all he stood for. 'We belonged nowhere' and 'learned to exploit our own insularity. Wherever we went abroad, we were strangers, but we were very knowing strangers.'

Louis MacNeice, the poet and broadcaster, whose father was a parish priest in Ulster and later a Bishop, expressed the sense of an abiding childhood influence when he wrote:

'. . . such remains my childhood's frame
Like a belated rock in the red Antrim clay
That cannot at this era change its pitch or name . . .'[15]

When his mother was in hospital his father 'sought escape from his grief and worry in overwork, and the children saw him less and less. Coming in at night, frequently cold and wet and always tired, he would kiss them, try to say something cheerful, and then retire to his study. Stallworthy, in his biography, said Louis in bed would hear him "intoning away, communing with God. And because of his conspiracy with God . . . was afraid of him"'.[16]

Like Raban, MacNeice, saw the hedge round his home as a barrier, but within it was his world, made sad by the death of his mother, and with limited social contact beyond. 'All this sadness and conflict and attrition and frustration were set in this one acre near the smoky town'.

MacNeice too saw his father in a new light as an adult.

'Who for all his responsibility compiled
Account books of a devout, precise routine
Kept something in him solitary and wild'.

His father's situation can also be seen in a wider context through the comments of the research clergy who said they would find it very difficult to continue in ministry if they were widowed. The implication in each case was not just the practical difficulty of bringing up children alone, but also the loss of companionship and support in such an isolated, largely unsupported job.

---

15 Raban, J. (1986) *Coasting*. London: Collins Harvill.
16 Longley, M. (ed.) (1988) *Louis MacNeice: Selected poems*. London: Faber and Faber.

The economist, Charles Handy, also spoke of the confined world of his childhood. He had thought of his father, rector of a small, rural Church of Ireland parish for 40 years, as a 'quiet and rather ordinary man, albeit kind and loving. He was unambitious, careful about money – careful because there wasn't much – punctilious in his work and sincere in his beliefs. He did not have much to do with the wealth-creating part of the world, or with its products. By the time I was eighteen I had resolved never to be poor, never to go to church again, and never to be content with where I stood in life. I went off in search of fame and fortune.'[17]

Success had a price. He was 'on the edge of big time, too busy to attend to my family. "Until I was ten", said my daughter years later, "I thought you were the man who came to lunch on Sundays"'. He does not say whether this reflected the working pattern of his father. After his father died he saw him differently. He was 'staggered by the numbers who came to say farewell to this quiet man, and the emotion which they showed. He had clearly affected the lives of hundreds of people in ways I had never imagined'. This is an interesting comment in the light of the Leadership Group's thoughts on success and failure.

One of the authors has counselled adult clergy children over many years, and it has been striking that adult clergy children of all denominations have expressed particular interest in our research. Their experiences too have suggested consistently that clergy families in the past were socially and physically isolated, and under severe financial pressure. They were also cut off from extended family because of time, distance and contrasting financial positions. The large house they lived in, usually impossible to heat, gave a false impression of their lifestyle and added to the isolation. They felt constantly observed, and under pressure to set an example in the congregation and in the wider parish.

IV. REFLECTIONS

Using the key issues from this valuable background information, we shall consider the effects of clergy families 'being seen as public figures

17 Stallworthy, J. (1995) *Louis MacNeice*. London: Faber and Faber.
18 Handy, C. (1997) *The Hungry Spirit Beyond Capitalism: A Quest for Purpose in the*

(and role models) essentially defined in terms of work for the purposes of almost all social contacts'. We shall look at congregations' awareness of the demands on clergy that this type of expectation creates and how family members react if they are expected to 'behave as if they had been appointed or were paid'.

Signs of physical or psychological illness shown in the families will be monitored, as well as isolation and stimulation. We shall note issues of intrusion into personal and family life, as well as restrictions for the family because of living in a specific, recognizable house in a particular area, and 'not having choice about the proportion of their income they could spend on housing'.

We shall look at any lack of balance in the job between demands, supports and restraints, and the availability of official support systems.

An issue, linked to the research on the police, is that clergy routinely have to minister to the families of those involved in sudden death, in hospital, at home and regularly at funeral services. We shall see whether clergy have easy access to peer-group support for this type of experience, or opportunity to discuss traumatic experiences in regular supervision. If not, we shall also consider whether there is evidence that 'expressing signs of stress could be considered personal and professional weakness' or lack of faith, and how 'failure to express traumatic experiences affects the family'. A linked issue will be whether clergy feel they have been 'heard and understood' when they discuss difficulties of any sort with senior clergy.

Throughout we shall think particularly of the statement by the Society of Mary and Martha that the problem of stress in clergy families 'belongs to us all', and the whole church needs to work on it together. 'The church cannot afford not to take better care of its clergy and they in turn must be accountable'. We shall bear in mind the need for honesty if there is to be the 'sea change' that is necessary to 'revitalize the church and its priesthood'.

Finally we shall think of the place of the clergy family and whether parishioners or the general public consider that there is 'no theological reason to assert that either marriage or ordination is more sacred than the other'.

5 Stress in a Family Setting

I. THE CONTEXT OF FAMILY STRESS AND THE IMPACT OF LIFE STAGES

We have been exploring key factors to bear in mind as we think about the issues of family stress, how this develops and accumulates and why it may be hard to address. We have outlined the main structures of Church life as a backdrop for understanding the context in which clergy families live and work, and the issues of being public figures. We have also considered the isolation for the families because of the public's uncertainty about the clergy role and how to relate to a clergy family. This uncertainty may be a two-way process, as the family also has to learn the best way to relate to those around them, as we saw in Jonathan Raban's experience as a clergy child in Chapter 4.

An early but helpful study relating to our thinking about clergy families emphasizes the 'haven function' of a family[1] in helping family members to cope with stress. It provides 'a safe place to relax and be oneself ... where one can set aside the burdens and demands of the outside world for as long as both the person and the family consider appropriate'. All families may not of course provide a 'haven', but it could be much more difficult for a clergy family if their home is seen as a part of the church where the public come for help.

Different stages in the life cycle of the family may bring their own particular issues of stress such as the birth of a baby, adolescence or a grandparent's illness and death. These will have a significant impact on the family. If they occur at different levels of the family at the same

---

Modern World. London: Hutchinson.

1   Caplan, G. (1976) 'The Family as a support system', In G. Caplan and M. Killilea (eds) *Support systems and mutual help: Multi-disciplinary explorations.* New York: Grune & Stratton.

time, there can be a 'quantum leap in anxiety'.[2] These factors are very important to the family but if their overall situation is not taken into account or even known about by bishops or parishioners, the family may then be blamed for not coping.

Different stages will happen too in a diocese or parish, for example, key church leaders changing or a bishop's illness or retirement. These may limit the support that is available to a priest or family at that time, and make other new demands much harder to handle. If two or three stressful stages come together in the family and the church situation, the stresses are not just added together but the 'leap in anxiety' is multiplied.

The Changing Family Life Cycle also suggests that 'symptoms (of stress) are most likely to appear when there is an interruption or dislocation in the unfolding family cycle',[3] such as long-term illness, making it hard to move on to the next stage. In the same way it may be hard for a diocese or the parish 'family' to move on after, say, the death in office of the bishop or incumbent, an affair or conviction, or a priest leaving prematurely.

These are highly sensitive issues. If they are not addressed and carefully managed, the diocese or parish may be left in a state of shock or bereavement, and issues for the next incumbent and his family may be overlooked. A priest's early stages in a parish may be doubly complicated unless they are told about the parish's recent history.

Bearing all these issues of context and family life stages in mind, two related models for defining and managing stress will help to give clear guidelines for exploring the complex nature of stress in a family.

II. THE ABCX MODEL[4]

This considers the interaction between four stages in the development of stress and how it may lead to crisis.

A. The event that is producing stress
B. The family's crisis-meeting resources if the pressure continues

2   Carter, E. and McGoldrick, M. ((1989) *The Changing Family Life Cycle – A Framework for Family Therapy.* Needham Heights, MA: Allyn and Bacon.
3   As n. 2 above.
4   Hill, R. (1958) Generic features of families under stress, in *Social Casework,* 49, 129–150.

C. The definition the family makes of the event. 'If the family defines the event as insurmountable, the likelihood of strain or crisis is much greater'

X. Crisis develops if efforts to master the stress are unsuccessful.

An example will help us to see why the family may define the event in this way. A family having a second or third child may say it is more difficult now to have meetings in the vicarage at the children's bedtime. If the situation is understood and another member offers their home as a venue, or suggests using the church hall, the family will feel more able to put down appropriate boundaries in future. The reaction may be, 'the vicarage has always been used and it will be very inconvenient or cold and uncomfortable to meet elsewhere'. The family may then hesitate in future to ask for the parish's support and understanding.

Most writers on stress suggest that if an individual or family feel they have some degree of choice and control over a situation, it makes a significant difference to the outcome. In this model 'coping' is seen as 'actions that make it possible for the family to understand, shape and master the environment as well as themselves', indicating a sense of control.

III. THE DOUBLE ABCX MODEL[5]

These ideas are extended in this model in response, not only to the initial stressful event, but also to the crisis. 'There appear to be at least five broad types of stressors and strains contributing to a pile-up in the family system in a crisis situation:

1. The initial stressful event and its hardships
2. Family life cycle events creating new demands
3. Prior strains such as care for an elderly parent
4. The consequences of family efforts to cope, which may involve financial hardship or time restraint

---

5   McCubbin, H. & Patterson, J. (1983a) The Family Stress Process: A double ABCX Model of adjustment and adaptation, in H. McCubbin, M. Sussman & J. Patterson (eds) *Advances and Developments in Family Stress Theory and Research.* New York: Hayworth Press.

5. Ambiguity, both within the family and socially, such as how much family interaction should be changed in adapting to the crisis, and how much others should be told about it.' This may be a particularly fine line to judge for the families of public figures.

The concern is with both short-term adjustment, and more long-term adaptation to restore balance.

IV. REFLECTIONS

Viewing stress in context in this way is particularly helpful in assessing the position of clergy families. Their situation may be assessed only in terms of the crisis by those outside the family, rather than within the wider framework of these models. The families may not find it easy to talk about all the issues they are facing, because of their public role or confidentiality. Walsh[6] reminds us that, 'it is crucial to assess each family's strengths and vulnerabilities in relation to their particular social and developmental contexts'. If individual factors are taken separately, the complexity of a situation and the cumulative effect of stress may be ignored, and the individual or family blamed for not coping.

When support systems in the parish or from wider family and friends are fragile or even absent, Walsh points out that there may be nobody to remind the family of their 'abilities and strengths which they may be doubting or which they have entirely forgotten'. We have frequently found that people may lose a sense of their capabilities in stressful situations. Reminding them of their strengths and resources in handling other situations can help them to see how these can be used in their present dilemma. This is one reason why comparisons can be so undermining because these focus on situations that other people face and their abilities, rather than the specific issues for this family at this time and their strengths in dealing with them.

The models explored above are still individual in the sense that they relate to how the individual family may cope with stress. Much more attention has been given in recent years to employment

6 Walsh, F. (1993) Conceptualisation of Normal Family Functioning, in F. Walsh (ed.) *Normal Family Processes* (2nd edn). London: Guilford Press.

practices and how these may become significant stressors for the family. In 2004 the Health and Safety Executive Code set specific standards for easing the pressure and improving the quality of life at work, and for increasing support of employees. The organization's response to stress, whether caused by work issues or not, may be crucial to a family's definition of a stressful event. As we saw in Chapter 4, the possibility of independence and self-determination are also linked to the organization's response. Even small changes in this response can make a significant difference to the 'pile-up in the family system in a crisis situation' mentioned in the Double ABCX model.

All these aspects of stress will be considered throughout the book.

6 Setting Up the Research

I. FINDING THE FAMILIES

We had now explored the setting for clergy families and had guidelines for considering stress within a family generally. Our aim was to have extensive discussions with a number of clergy families to understand their experiences in the family as a whole. We wanted them to meet two criteria. They should be able to meet with us three times at yearly intervals with all family members present, and they should not be in the midst of a crisis or receiving counselling for stress. This would give us an understanding of issues they faced in the general run of clergy family life.

We wrote to the bishops of four dioceses across England to ask if we could approach families in their area. Each diocese had several different types of parish. We also had friends in those areas to provide a base while we carried out our interviews.

The process that followed was revealing. In two dioceses the bishop passed our request to an appropriate member of his staff who talked through the research with us and then contacted some families who met our criteria. In less than a month a number of families had agreed to take part.

In the other two dioceses the papers were passed from department to department, with considerable delays in between. We had to track their progress with further calls and it took almost a year to be given permission to recruit families. This was a significant delay, especially for research that had a span of over three years just to gather the information before the analysis could begin.

At length this process produced 20 families from the four dioceses. The staff members in each diocese who put their names forward would have known all clergy in their diocese. They considered the families they contacted came well within our research criteria and were not seen by diocesan staff as families with problems. One official wrote to the families in his diocese, 'The fact that you are receiving this letter is proof positive that you are considered a normal family!'

All 20 families took part in the first two rounds of interviews. Just one family declined to do the third interview as they felt it was a difficult moment for them to take part. All the other 19 families completed the three interviews, despite the extended time commitment.

II. THE REFERENCE GROUPS

We also set up two Reference Groups whose purpose was twofold: first, we wanted them to comment after each round of interviews on what the families said; secondly we wanted to understand more of the broader issues surrounding the families' situation. We would also explore concerns or difficulties that the Group members had in their pastoral or management roles with clergy families.

The six members of each Group came from different dioceses from the families and all had lived or worked in one or more other dioceses previously, adding to their range of experience. Their names were suggested to us by a variety of sources including bishops and laity. All members had a particular interest or involvement in the care of clergy and their families. Each Group met for a day on three occasions following each round of interviews. Like the families, they were therefore part of a process of data gathering and reflection.

We greatly appreciated that members who carry great responsibility within the wider Church gave so much time to our research, especially the three bishops. Naturally the views they expressed were personal rather than representing any official position. Nevertheless, their broad range of perspectives from the different parts of the system was a significant contribution in helping us to build a rounded picture of stress issues for clergy families.

1. The Pastoral Care Group

The Pastoral Group was made up of three women and three men involved in counselling clergy and/or their families. Three of these held specialist remits: one was a diocesan director of Pastoral Care and Counselling, another dealt with divorced or separated clergy wives, another was a theological college pastoral tutor. They brought diverse experiences of the issue of clergy family stress across the whole range of a priest's career.

2. The Leadership and Management Group

Three bishops, a college principal, an archdeacon, and an Archbishop's staff member in contact with clergy from all over the country, formed the Leadership Group. They brought a very wide knowledge of Church structures and organizational issues affecting clergy. Two of the bishops said they had joined the Group to learn as well as to contribute. The college principal said this was the first time he had known a principal and bishops sit down together to discuss clergy family stress.

The families and all Group members were assured that their identity would remain strictly confidential.

III. RESEARCH METHODOLOGY

1. The focus of the research

For many people this is a very important issue and helps them to assess whether the research is valid so we will outline the way we worked. We would be interviewing whole families rather than individuals, and we were aware of 'the importance of a match between the information we were seeking and the way this was gathered, analysed and reported'.[1] Our aim was to look at the families' understanding of the different aspects of their life and relationships, and how these fitted together into an overall perspective.

We had looked at the structures of the Church as the wider context for clergy and their families. In addition the personal context for each family sets the scene for their relationships within the community, such as schools, health systems and friendship networks, and the way these influence their ongoing lives. How were these links and relationships built up and what might make them change? We wanted to understand the meaning the families gave to interactions within the parish as a whole and not just within the church.

We realized the most appropriate framework or paradigm would be an open-ended, interpretive approach[2] with no preconceived ideas

---

1   Marshall, C. (1985) 'Appropriate criteria for trustworthiness and goodness for qualitative research on education organizations', in *Quality and Quantity* 19(4) 353–373.
2   Costain Schou, K. & Hewison, J. (1994) 'Issues of Interpretive Methodology', in *Human Systems,* 5, 1–2, 45–69.

about the research outcome. We would also gather information from the families using an in-depth qualitative approach. This would involve a shared search with the families for meaning in their context. We felt this would be more in keeping with our aim than a quantitative approach, which uses statistics from a larger sample and compares the findings with those from a control group. As it would be the first study of this type on clergy *families*, we felt it was important to understand the underlying issues for them in their 'unique and specific context', rather than doing a comparative study at this stage. The issue of comparisons and context will be raised specifically in Chapter 19.

2. Interviewing whole families

Having chosen the most appropriate way of conducting the research, we knew from our training and experience that the Milan approach to family interviews would enable us to gather information from the families using, a respectful, open stance. The Milan approach has in fact been likened to a 'research operation engaged in … with the family'[3] and it has also been shown specifically how the techniques are immediately transferable to a research context.[4]

Families need a different approach from talking to an individual. If the interviewer speaks to each person in turn, it may be difficult to keep the rest of the family involved. The children in particular might well 'switch off' as they have 'heard it all before'. It is important to maintain their interest and curiosity.

How does the interview happen? Whenever possible interviewers work in a team to provide other perspectives in discussion. The team develops hypotheses based on their knowledge of families generally and on any information about the family's particular circumstances, and questions are built around these. Subsequent questions are linked to the family's replies and this gives a flow and coherence to the interview.

There is no attempt to prove the hypotheses in this type of

---

3   Boscolo, L., Cechin, G., Hoffman, L. & Penn, P. (1987) *Milan Systemic Family Therapy*. New York: Basic Books.

4   Burck, C. (2005) 'Comparing qualitative research methodologies for systemic research: the use of grounded theory, discourse analysis and narrative analysis', in *The Journal of Family Therapy* 27, 3, 237–262.

research. The aim is to use them to provide a focus to the session and to gather information. They can be changed if they no longer seem relevant and are not producing anything new. The hypotheses are not shared with the families. This was an important issue for both of the Reference Groups. When they saw the intensity of the cycle of stress that the families experienced they asked if we had fed in information, and we were able to explain how open both the hypotheses and questions were.

The interviewer may also ask one family member their views on relationships and events involving other members. This is a fascinating technique as the family, especially children and young people are curious to hear what someone else will say. 'Why did Mum think we were upset?' 'Has Dad cottoned on that the churchwardens are always criticizing us?' All members will want to agree or disagree or add something more. This gives indications of mutual understanding and support, freedom to differ and encouragement to children to be quite open. It also means that the technique has inbuilt checks and counterchecks against one person's voice dominating the session, or the interviewer being stuck with one explanation, and ensures that everyone's views will be heard. Observing how these issues are dealt with in practice becomes part of the overall information about the families themselves.

At times the issues we were exploring involved deep pain, and we were left wondering what we would find when we returned a year later for the second or third rounds of interviews. Throughout we were struck by the families' resilience, commitment and faith. There was also much laughter and fun in the midst of serious discussion.

The children were remarkably perceptive and often the parents were surprised and touched by their awareness and concern. They also seemed to feel free at times to make observations that may have been difficult for the parents to hear but the comments did not have a sense of blame.

The three interviews helped us to compare the families' perspectives at different periods in their current lives and note contradictions and variations. They also helped us to 'capture the complexity'[5] of the family's situation more readily than a single

---

5 Strauss, A. L. (1987) *Qualitative analysis for social scientists*. Cambridge: Cambridge University Press.

interview. Our work with the families over three years gave us 90 hours of in-depth recorded interviews, a rich and diverse resource for qualitative work of this nature.

Once the interviews were complete, we considered Grounded Theory would be the most appropriate system for analysing the information we had gained. This again has a carefully planned system with inbuilt checks, which dovetails with the Milan interviews. We transcribed the 90 hours of the tapes ourselves, which gave us the 'constant interaction with the data' central to Grounded Theory. We also summarized the main themes for the Groups after each round of interviews. This meant we revisited all that the families had said on four or five separate occasions so we were able to check and recheck emerging themes at each stage.

A final part of the process with the Milan approach is to look for a unifying theme to link the whole system, and connect all parts of what the families have said. In the same way Grounded Theory develops a 'storyline' which makes these connections and brings a wholeness to the end result.

IV. REFLECTIONS

We gained a great respect for everyone who took part. Within our long experience of family interviews we found the families as a whole and all other participants were particularly open about the joys and privileges of clergy family life as well as the dilemmas they faced. Without this openness the result would have been much less dynamic.

'Going with the system' in each diocese gave us an unexpected insight into the difficulties clergy or parishes face if correspondence with diocesan staff is unclear or delayed, and the potential stress this could cause. Especially for newer clergy, unsure of the system, they may be left in a vacuum if they do not have an adequate reply to what, for them, is an important question. The dioceses we contacted appeared to have very different cultures and patterns of teamwork.

Within the whole research we were able to use our background knowledge and experience, as Strauss[6] suggests, to 'be aware of

6   See n. 5 above.

subtleties of meaning', and to 'understand events and actions more quickly'. But there must be a balance. He also reminds us to 'challenge assumptions, experience and knowledge' as this can 'block you from seeing things that have become routine or obvious'. Using these criteria from Grounded Theory helped us to 'step back and critically analyse situations, recognize and avoid bias, obtain valid and reliable data and to think analytically'.[7]

How will our work relate to the findings of other researchers? Ideally it will be part of an ongoing conversation between versions produced by different researchers with differing perspectives as Morgan[8] suggests, rather than looking for consensus. A different perspective need not disprove an earlier one; rather, it becomes part of building up knowledge. We hope this ongoing conversation will help in addressing the overall dilemma raised in Chapter 1.

7 Strauss, A. L. and Corbin, J. (1990) *Basics of Qualitative Research: Grounded Theory procedures and techniques*. Newbury Park, CA: Sage.

8 Morgan, G. (ed.) (1983) *Beyond Method: Strategies for Social Research*. London: Sage.

PART THREE
The Curacy Stage: The First Family Interviews

7 Moves, Accommodation and Education

I. THE FIRST INTERVIEWS

We had now prepared the background, and we arranged to meet the families in their homes at a time when all members could be present.

In this interview we followed the family's experience from the decision to go forward for ordination to the priest's first appointment as vicar. At these training and curacy stages, the priest and the family are being introduced to the ecclesiastical system with all the changes in lifestyle involved, although some were married after the training stage. They are also establishing an understanding of the informal as well as the formal rules of the job.

We concentrated on how this understanding was affected by two issues for the families: communication; and support, both in the job and for the family. Difficulties in either of these areas would affect most aspects of the families' lives and could cause stress. If communication was poor or the appropriate channels for discussion were unclear or blocked, then it would be harder for them to know what the rules were.

Within these broad issues we knew that stress was often centred round practical concerns, in particular children's education and the family's accommodation, so general practical issues were noted.

This took up to an hour. We then traced their family tree on the flip chart. Younger children, who might not have known issues their parents had faced during theological training or curacies, became closely involved. They enjoyed telling us about aunts and uncles, cousins and grandparents and how often they saw them. The aim of the family tree was to see the clergy family in the context of their extended family and the extent of mutual support and communication, as well as seeing them within their parish and diocesan system.

The families' discussions highlighted their deep sense of faith, commitment and resilience during the upheavals of the early years before a priest is appointed to an incumbency and is responsible for a parish. When ordinands finish their training, they and their families frequently experienced confusion and uncertainty in many areas of their lives. The data showed that they felt undervalued both personally and professionally. Their family needs might be sidelined or made subordinate to principles decided at parish level, without a check being made on the families' overall position. The situation was intensified during life stages in the family or the Church.

The families attempted to make appropriate decisions affecting all members with little information and few if any guidelines. They often felt they had little control over a whole range of issues they had to handle, especially moves, education and accommodation. Dovetailing the family's needs and possible complications in all three areas made this stage particularly difficult.

They might find the job described to them at interview was very different to the job on the ground. The pressure to conform was exerted in a wide variety of ways both by congregations and the public. The messages might be from individuals or groups and were frequently contradictory. However the strongest message was that the job must come first.

II.   MOVES

Moves come high on any stress scale and involve a wide range of significant losses for all members of the family. They leave behind their friendship and support networks, a sense of knowing and trusting practical services such as GPs, schools and many more. One partner may lose a job. Previous losses for the family or for individual members may bring echoes of pain that give a move added difficulty.

1.   The first step

The families of ordinands training at college face at least three moves in six or seven years. They leave their own home to live near college, move to a curacy and then to a first parish as vicar. Each move involves selling their house and possibly buying again, or negotiating rented or clergy housing as well as many other changes. Those training on a local theological course will also be leaving an established family situation as they take up a curacy. Most of the research clergy were looking back at their experience of this stage, and for several of them this would have meant having two curacies involving yet another move.

One family's move to college was particularly traumatic. Just as the ordinand was due to begin his training the housing market dipped. Rather than sell the house the family stayed where they were while he lived for six weeks with a vicar near college. They then let their home, and rented a spare clergy house in a local parish.

His wife, who had been born where they lived, left her 'very close' family of mother and four sisters behind for the first time. She agreed with her husband that the college wives group was very welcoming, 'once you got into it'. Nevertheless, she described the experience as 'a move into nothingness'.

The parents had originally minimized the pain and anxiety it had clearly caused them and said that their second son was too young to be affected by the move. Later the son talked of moving from infant school to a 'posh Year 3 class with nice desks' in a junior school for those six weeks before the move. Then he went to a middle school with ordinary desks near college and then back to another junior school for his father's first curacy. Each stage, he felt, was 'a step down'. The fixed memories not only of the desks but also of their first cold night as tenants in the clergy house near college, having left their centrally heated home, seemed to illustrate the bleakness of their experience.

Another husband went to college while his family stayed in their original home. He said he might manage to get lifts home for two or three nights a week but his wife said their family life was disjointed. They could not plan ahead and she was left with a lot more ferrying of their four children while he was away. They were very short of money. Others described a variety of similar experiences.

2. The move to a curacy

For three to four days before their ordination weekend, ordinands are on retreat, possibly some distance from their new parish. This is a solemn time of spiritual preparation. Their spouses, who are left to cope alone with the family and all the practical issues of moving, would not feel able to interrupt them unless a situation were critical.

One man said that fellow ordinands had all discussed the move at the end of college. There was no more stressful way of creating tension within a family than expecting people to leave college and their friends, take up a new job the next weekend, be ordained into something quite new at the heart of a parish and move into a new house in a new area so that the whole family was uprooted. Children would also be moving schools. 'All the stresses, all are there'. In addition the ordinands would just have had the pressure of final exams for their theological degree.

For another ordinand the parish's agenda came before the family's needs. The PCC decided on principle, that money for alterations to the curate's house should be raised before the alterations began. The house was therefore not ready for the family. They had to move into another house for over four months while the alterations were finished, and then move again. The ordinand had worked for an international company and the family had many moves in the previous 18 years. Now with four children between five and 15, this family was faced with additional disruption, unable to unpack their belongings for an unpredictable length of time. In her book on Army families, Jolly[1] points out that no matter how many times a family has moved, the stress is still high. Military accommodation of course would be available and checked before occupation.

3. Here we go again

Another move is always on the horizon. 'From the word go your day of departure is one day nearer each day', one priest said. 'With a curacy it is moulded in your mind, there is an inevitability about your move'. The children, in particular, find that inevitability so difficult. They live with it for three or four years having already faced it if the priest has trained at college.

Teenagers from three families spoke of their sense of 'devastation' at the prospect of another move so soon. 'You don't want to get too close to somebody because you know that sooner or later you'll be moving on.'

Another said that all her friends, in fact her whole life was there, but it all seemed pointless if they were moving. Two sisters from a third family echoed these feelings of suspense and uncertainty. It was

---

1   Jolly, R. (1987) *Military Man, Family Man: Crown Property?* London: Brassey's Defence Publishers.

several months before they knew that their present school and all their friends would be within reach of the new parish.

Parents told us how a younger child had overheard a conversation about moving, and thought he was concerned at a deeper level about when they would move again. 'Will we be here next week? Should we get some cardboard boxes to start packing my toys?'

The anxieties experienced by children may vary according to their age when a move takes place. They all spoke of their fears of what new schools and new areas would be like, whether the work would be harder, and what new friendships they would make. In their book *Stress and Work*[2] the authors suggest that 'certain age groups are more susceptible' to the stress of moves. 'Pre-school children experience feelings of loss and insecurity. They may even interpret a move as a form of punishment. A young child may revert to infantile behaviour such as thumb sucking and bed-wetting or may experience more nightmares. Children in junior school may experience similar feelings of insecurity but teenagers, to whom peer approval and relationships are so important, frequently have a particularly difficult time'.

The sense of loss is there for partners too. At a clergy wives' conference on bereavement that one of the authors attended, a member said that she felt bereaved when they moved from their previous parish. Suddenly the whole conference came alive as one after another spoke of similar experiences.

The parents, as well as facing their own adjustments, expressed both concern that moves should be right for the whole family and guilt that their decision about ordination should cause so much disruption for their children.

III. ACCOMMODATION

Moves and accommodation were closely linked. The families are expected to move to an existing curate's house, which usually has three small bedrooms with one bedroom needed as a study. If older ordinands ask for the house to be changed because it is too small for a family with teenage children, this can cause a range of difficulties.

---

2   Ivancevich, J. and Matteson, P. (1980) *Stress and Work: a managerial perspective.* Glenview, Ill: Scott, Foresman.

The families' comments about housing have to be seen in the context of their home being the centre of the priest's work with frequent phone calls and visitors at any hour.

1. Somewhere to live

One family said everything had gone well at the first interview for the curacy but they thought it would be impractical to live in the existing curate's house with two boys approaching adolescence. 'There was basically one room downstairs, just over 10 by 12 feet, and a kitchen which would not even take a washing machine'. They were assured at that stage, both verbally and in writing, that the house would be changed. The parish knew that the previous curate, with only one younger child, had found the house very difficult to live in as a clergy house.

During the process that followed, housing arrangements fell through three times. They were not told what was happening, possibly, they thought, because people had not wanted to worry them. They did not want to sign contracts for the sale of their own house if they had nowhere to move to. With three weeks to go 'we came and started putting our foot down' with the vicar.

'The previous week the Parish Church Council (PCC) had discussed whether, as no house had been found, God might be saying that they should not sell the old house but we should go into it. It went to a vote and they decided that wasn't the truth.' Otherwise 'we just would not have gone'.

The question remained of how many of the PCC still thought the original house should have been retained, and what resentments or negative impressions might be left by the couple's 'demand'. The question of course could have no answer.

Four-bedroom houses were for sale. The wife said 'the decision had been that it wouldn't look good for curates to have houses that were too big and anyway it was good for the soul for curates to ... That was said by the person with responsibility for finding a house but whether it was said in jest ... And comments that the curate's house was on every agenda of the PCC as well as there being a certain feeling that we'd caused them a lot of bother'.

A churchwarden and 'one or two people' had written or apologized that the family had been 'caused so much bother'. The couple thought the majority had been totally unaware of what was happening, apart from weekly prayer requests in the church newsletter.

Finally the family spent eleven weeks in rented accommodation with their furniture in store. The vicar went on holiday the day they moved into the new house. 'So I was left ... for the first time in the parish on my own. And I left the family surrounded by packing cases. If I'd said, "I can't cope", he was the sort of man who would probably have cancelled his holiday'.

At different stages this mature couple had felt 'embarrassed', 'torn apart because we felt it was the right place', and 'angry with them all that they hadn't been able to appreciate that college is stressful anyway, coupled with not having somewhere to live', and all the other changes for the whole family.

The end result was that 'it took us a year to recover. We don't talk about it so much now. It depends what "getting over it" means. There wasn't anyone in particular we could blame. A year later my report to my bishop said basically that I'd not managed in that year to find any time for family, full stop.'

Their sons knew their parents were anxious. 'It was more tense in the house. They were more jumpy and on edge and argued more'. The boys said they worried because of the tension, causing a cycle of stress.

2. A two bedroom house and isolation

The issues of accommodation are particularly linked to a clergyman's home being a working house and also to one of the bedrooms having to be a study. This effectively reduces the recommended size of a curate's house to two bedrooms. If the curate has an adequate office in the church, a study might be less necessary. The families' comments suggested that curates might well be finishing or going over sermons on a Saturday evening so there would still be times when they needed study space at home.

The house finally chosen for the couple with the two sons nearing teenage had a sitting room just over 10 feet square and a second smaller room attached to a galley kitchen. The study in the church, promised by the PCC as part of a refurbishment plan, 'never happened. We were automatically forced into making one of the bedrooms into a study.' They added, 'we used to have friends to stay for weekends but it never happens now. We've had family to stay here twice but it's very, very difficult to fit everybody in.'

More will be said about the sense of personal and professional isolation frequently mentioned by the families. For this couple the restriction on seeing their wider family and losing contact with friends would have added to this sense of isolation.

3. All in together

Another family had to use one of the two downstairs rooms as a study, leaving the remaining room for the family. They had children of different ages and both sexes. One of the teenagers had to share with a much younger brother so the only place he could study in the evening was in the family room.

His father said that such a small house felt claustrophobic for five people. It was not so bad if you had a one-way system. 'And all moved round the house by numbers', his wife added. 'Sometimes we have collision courses, not just physically but also emotionally'.

'They were thrown in together and that's been difficult for them, very difficult really', a father said of his teenage daughters in one of the smallest houses. 'Even at college we had our own house so they had separate rooms and their own space.' In contrast a family with four children in a larger than usual curate's house said it had probably made one of the biggest differences to the family.

4. Attention to detail

One couple moved to a curacy as they married. The house was damp. After six months the parish spent £100 on having a leaking pipe put right and ... 'it made all the difference'. Several families echoed that same phrase about a number of issues. Attention to details, large and small, which seemed unimportant to parishioners or the diocese, could 'make all the difference' to the families.

5. The Reference Groups' comments

The Pastoral Group mentioned three assumptions, which might be made by the hierarchy, the parish or the general public:

- The parish knew the family's needs
- Clergy were privileged because they were protected from mortgages and responsibility for maintenance
- The vocation was for the whole family.

The Group thought the family's perception might be quite different. They spoke of the importance of people feeling comfortable in their surroundings, and said ordinands should 'say very clearly at an early stage what was appropriate for the family in terms of housing'. They mentioned that this depended on 'ordinands' authority and ability to be honest about their needs'. These comments seemed to give *ordinands* the responsibility to ensure that their housing was adequate. The couple in III.1 above had said from the start that the house was inadequate and had shown the independence the Leadership Group recommended. Even so, a few people at the heart of the congregation seemed to have an idea of how the curate should be perceived, and what was 'good for his soul' and in the end their view prevailed.

The Leadership Group also felt there was pressure from lay people for curates to live in 'the same sort of housing', which meant a three-bedroom house with one as a study. They thought pressure on the family of a house of this size would be less if children were under five. A later comment, however, that 'when the priest was coping with failure, the children would suffer because they would be scapegoats', would presumably include very young children.

IV. EDUCATION

The choice of a parish was the dominant factor at the end of training and after a curacy, but a close second was the children's education.

1. An early move

In the Church of England ordinations traditionally take place in the ordinand's new diocese on St Peter's Day, the last weekend of June. The children therefore have to leave their schools three to four weeks early and miss the end of year activities.

One family wanted their boys to feel at home with their schools before the summer rather than spending the holidays wondering if they would fit in. The younger one in particular was 'a worrier'. An eleven-year-old went to a new junior school in July before moving to a comprehensive school in September. 'I had to make some friends quickly here. And some things were half finished that I left behind.' Counsellors emphasize the importance of good endings but for her there was no proper ending not only to that year but also to her time at junior school. The younger daughter went to senior school a year later. Her father spoke of her struggle to overcome the nervousness associated with moving to two new schools in two years. He thought she sometimes reflected the pressures that so many moves put on all of them.

Their comments showed how anxiety might be expressed within the family when stress built up. Her father realized that sometimes he and his wife started the arguments but added, 'When we're all tense, our younger daughter is quite often the first to explode, whereas all of us probably want to, so she acts as a safety valve. She starts us off, she'll be the trigger and involves us all in having a good blow up'.

2. Which school?

The couples were considering jobs all over the country and often had a long journey to the parish when they were looking for a curacy. They spoke of always seeming to be short of time to gather information because there was so much to discuss and arrange.

A family on an inner-city estate chose a church comprehensive school for their son but this choice can mean clergy children are the only ones, as he was, from that estate or area at that school. This may isolate them from local friendship networks. If they go to the local school, as will be seen for vicar's children, they may be identified with their parent's job and be victimized.

For younger children the decision can be easier, especially if there is a church school that seems right for the individual child. One couple said that if they had decided it was the wrong school, it might have been very difficult. This echoed the comment of one vicar that he offended his churchwardens and others in his parish by making an alternative choice.

3. Timing of exams and staying behind

As GCSE and A-level courses take two years each and courses are not necessarily the same across the country, it is important for children to remain at the same school for those two years.

Two families with teenagers each had one child choosing options towards the end of Year 9, one taking GCSE and a third doing A-levels, all in the same year, as well as 'making university applications and all that pressure'. One of these children had to negotiate options 150 miles away before a move. In two families, teenagers changed to a different school or sixth form college for A-levels, leaving all their previous friends. Several children had three schools in four years.

Issues of the education of teenage children seemed to be considered only if curates raised them with the bishop. At such an early stage of their careers they were hesitant to do this, not wanting to 'demand, but to ask if adjustments could be made'. Of the four families still at the curacy stage at the beginning of the interviews, two negotiated a year's extension to their curacy. One had to renegotiate this with the same bishop when he queried it during their third year. The three teenagers in the other family thought their parents would have preferred not to stay. They had enjoyed the parish but there had been a mismatch with the Rector in terms of approach to worship and priorities for ministry, so an extra year was not easy to handle. A third family moved nearby so the children were able to remain at the same school. For the children in a fourth family, equally adamant that they did not want to move away, the priest's best efforts to stay in the area failed and he accepted a job in another part of the country.

One curate was told the family would have to leave at the beginning of May in the third year so that the house could be prepared for a successor. The son was taking his GCSE that year during May and June. Discussion at parish level brought an impasse and it was only after the curate had involved the bishop that agreement was reached for the family to stay until the exams were completed. It seemed ironic that this was one of the families who had had to live in temporary accommodation for several weeks because the house had not been ready for them.

The family who had to move to theological college after the October half term because of housing problems faced the whole range of possible complications over education. When they arrived, 'All the rest of the class had had half a term to settle in and were already in established groups'. Both children changed systems, one from lower to junior school, the other from middle school to comprehensive. The priest had two curacies so they moved twice more. Between curacies the older brother had to stay behind from May to July and live with the vicar in order to take his GCSE and finish the year. He therefore had no immediate parental support at a crucial time.

All the disruption caught up with the younger son who had previously described the desks in his different schools. He had to re-sit his GCSE. The timing of his exams now no longer fitted, as planned, with the move to an incumbency. He was left behind for the second year of his A-levels. He spoke of 'having to adjust in three ways: to my parents' move, to being left behind by my peers who went to university a year before I did, and to living in a family with small children while I studied'.

The second child in another family had to stay behind for a full year to complete her GCSE when her father left theological college. She was 15. She lived with a family she did not know well who did not have children. She gave a light-hearted account of how she missed her brothers and sister and 'not being able to shout at anybody. If I felt angry, I couldn't say anything. I had to just keep swallowing down and be trampled on. I couldn't even say anything about the food just, "Oh, that was lovely, thank you", rather than "Yuk!"'

Behind the laughter there had obviously been significant emotional adjustments for the parents and young people in both these families during these periods apart. They had originally planned a monthly visit for the daughter. It was soon obvious that this was not enough and it became a fortnightly routine. When she returned home for her A-levels, her new-found independence meant still more adjustments. There was a considerable financial implication not only in contributing to housekeeping expenses for her, but also for travelling home. Given the minimal budgets the families had at college and the restrictions of a curate's stipend, this was an added strain.

4.   Bullying and changing relationships

'Bullying and so forth' could be harder to deal with in the midst of so much change and insecurity. One father said his son had not told him for some time that he was being bullied.

Several of the girls spoke of the fickle, changing relationships with their friends. One daughter said, 'I've had a bit of trouble with my friends at school. They keep going off with each other and leaving me out and then they'll come back and be friends'. Her mother felt this was 'girls all over' but this did not take away from the stress when coupled with all the moves.

Additional losses that could occur in any friendship were added to the anxiety of moves. One girl said that two friends had moved away from the area in the previous year and all her other friends were now in another class. She had come to the school two years before and faced another move in a year so this was a very difficult loss.

5. The Reference Groups' comments

The discussion in the Pastoral Group about education centred on clergy children's experience of bullying by contemporaries, and expectations from teachers. They also thought the public's perception was that the children would be 'virtuous and meek and mild'. Children needed to talk about these things, but one member who had worked a lot with clergy children thought they would not want to make their parents feel guilty. They might feel disloyal and say nothing if the difficulties were linked to their parent's job.

The Leadership Group raised the question of timing in relation to children's A-levels and GCSEs, as these were a factor in planning moves. Four-year curacies could give flexibility. They felt that the needs of the family should be monitored in the parish, and suitable provision made for children. They did not suggest whether this should be the churchwardens' responsibility or how feedback would be given.

They thought the ideology of the parents might not be appropriate; for instance they might believe that their children should be educated locally even though this meant they were the only non-member of a particular ethnic or social group in that class or school. Urban church schools could then be a resource.

In a village they felt that what happens in the school could influence all of the priest's relationships. They also commented that the priest might be the only working person from the community who was not commuting, so might feel cut off from the local culture working at home in the study – an aspect of isolation.

V. REFLECTIONS

Many of the issues the families faced would be similar to those for any parents with jobs requiring frequent moves. However, the clergy families faced additional pressures linked both to their public role and having to live in a specific house in a specific area.

In the past, curates went straight from university to theological college. When they arrived in their first curacy, they were viewed as students in need of total training and housed accordingly. Those responsible for housing decisions within a parish now need to take into account the position of older ordinands and their children, and consider the long-term impact on the families of living in inadequate accommodation at the heart of a pressurized job, in the midst of several years of changing circumstances. Having their own space could give the children, especially the teenagers, some sense of security in at least one aspect of their lives.

More mature ordinands may need to spend time and effort caring for their parents. If they live at a distance, they would need to have their parents to stay as the clergy family could only visit them during their holidays.

In both parishes where the family had to move into temporary accommodation, the problem was not an issue of finance as such, but a question of principle. We have frequently been told, in counselling and personally, of many such instances. Primarily these have been due to a lack of forward planning by the parish. One difficulty is that curate's housing is provided by the parish, not, as for incumbents, by the diocese. If such vital issues for the family are left in the hands of busy lay members of the church, and according to the principles of a few individuals, then similar problems will continue to occur.

It seemed that parents might not receive support or understanding from different levels of the church about children's educational requirements. These would include the importance of finding new posts within a given area if possible to limit school changes, congregational pressure in terms of church schools, or being asked to move before GCSEs were complete. Even when parents made independent decisions in their children's best interests, this could lead to isolation for the children from either school or local friendship support.

The families were often bewildered by this lack of understanding from parishioners or diocesan staff, and by unrealistic expectations from all sources. Having given up many aspects of their lives for ordination, they had anticipated a response of reciprocal care and concern from within the Church as a whole. Instead their efforts to find their right way forward were often challenged or misconstrued. People at all levels looked at individual issues rather than seeing how these fitted into the families' whole situation.

In all three meetings the Reference Groups said that there should be a mutuality of care, particularly from the churchwardens, as well as local monitoring. This would still not give protection from principles and whims of parish members whose opinion might carry the day. Local monitoring did not seem to affect good practice on curates' housing.

8 The Public View of Curates

I. FINDING A CURACY

1. An accurate impression of the job

In their search for a curacy the couples felt they needed a parish's goals and their own to have a reasonable 'fit'. It was often not clear who had drawn up the job description, and information given at an interview might differ from this basic information. The ordinands seemed to have had varying guidance for teasing out the different goals and priorities that vicars, churchwardens, the PCC or other groups within the church might have.

The ordinand might meet a number of people during a visit to the parish and what they said would naturally reflect their own thoughts and concerns. Some students had been given specific guidelines by their tutors such as 'Choose the man' because the 'reasonable fit' must be primarily with the vicar as well as with the parish. They could get an impression in three ways: from meeting him; from observing others' reactions to him; and above all from the current curate.

One man said his predecessor in the post had almost nothing good to say about the vicar. This curate told him he must stand up for himself, say exactly what he meant and that he would be psychologically analysed at every turn. He found this a helpful warning. However, he felt it was an area of advice that tutors might need to readdress. If someone had sufficient life experience and could evaluate that curate's perspective, it was probably helpful, but someone with little other experience might be put off by such a reaction. Again a focus principally on the vicar might mean that students did not explore the wider issues of the parish.

The experience of students when they visited a parish could also be very different to the impression given by bishops. One student only discovered that the incumbent and his wife had recently separated when he arrived for his interview. The bishop had not mentioned this important detail.

'The choice of curacy is a very, very hard decision', one wife said. 'You receive the initial details about the parish and your husband might go on his own first. Then you visit it just once or possibly one other time as a couple or a family, and perhaps go to the church on one occasion and on that you have to decide, hopefully, prayerfully, trusting that you make the right decision.'

Almost all the couples spoke of it being a joint decision as the house as well as other family considerations were an integral part of such a decision. All the wives, regardless of churchmanship, intended to give some level of support to their husbands. They naturally wanted to know that their perspective had at least a reasonable fit with that particular church's culture. Even for a spouse who did not intend to be involved, a fit, in terms of a general acceptance of her intention, would be important to save misunderstandings later.

2. Contracts or taken on trust?

A student was given a work profile that had been right for the two previous curates. The vicar said it could be flexible, as each person brought individual talents to the job. Had it been more or less right for him? He laughed. 'Less rather than more', he thought.

Another student said that both the churchwardens and the vicar had been very open and the vicar had been quite specific about what he was offering. He also gave the student his own c.v. The student had been used to looking at these in his secular job. He had been able to 'ferret out' a number of things hidden in it and put the vicar on the spot as well as vice versa. Over the next three years he discovered that the initial presentation was different to the practice. The vicar said, for example, that he was non-directive, but at times was quite the opposite.

One man in his late thirties had had 17 years in industry with considerable experience of personnel issues. During his theological training he had been allocated to a placement parish where there had been conflict between the vicar and curate. As he talked to the vicar, the student realized that he had had nowhere to discuss and resolve very difficult experiences in both his own curacies, and had taken the trauma of those experiences into the relationship with a curate of his own. As a result, the ordinand had been particularly aware of needing to make a careful choice of curacy to avoid such a situation, but found himself in just such a position now. He felt he and his vicar had tested each other out but had very different ideas of how the job description should be fulfilled. The endless demands and expectations had led to an impossible workload, reflecting the vicar's own work style. After 18 months he felt the need to address this with the vicar and PCC who, in principle, were supportive. When we asked the family what differences they had noticed since then, the family all said they thought there'd been no change and his daughter added, 'If anything, he goes to more meetings than before'. He also experienced disapproval from some parish groups for raising the difficulties.

Both the pressure and the reactions had led to a lot of heartache for the family. His wife said it was a very useful experience to sort out so many things in a curacy. Her husband, however, said his concern would be that they should not leave the parish feeling wounded and take this with them, like the vicar he worked with at college. Our interview with the family seemed to be the first opportunity they had to talk freely about these difficulties. This curate, as a previous senior manager himself, was one who spoke at a later stage of the importance of supervision.

In each of these cases, and particularly the last, the couples had tried to understand the expectations and tasks of the job through focused discussion. Yet they had not been able to establish these with any sort of accuracy, despite their own maturity and insights.

3. The Psychological Contract

The ideas behind the Psychological Contract, described by Herriot and Pemberton,[1] help to clarify the difficulties curates face. The authors see the contract of employment as a four-stage process. First, each side feeds in information about what they are looking for and what they can offer so they can see whether the other side wants what they are offering. This leads to a negotiating stage with more specific offers from either party, leading to a contract. The contract is then monitored for change in either party's wants, to check that the contract is fair and is being kept. The process then allows for

---

1 Herriot, P. and Pemberton, C. (1995) *New Deals: The Revolution in Managerial Careers.* Chichester: Wiley.

renegotiation or termination. They suggest that the advantage of the model is that it can be applied diagnostically to discover at which stage of the process difficulties are occurring. They point out that there may be marked differences in the perceptions of the contract by the two parties so 'actions based upon an assumed shared contract may be sadly mistaken'.

This dilemma is highlighted for curates who in *all* cases found that their verbal arrangement with their training vicar was different to the 'contract' they thought they had made. As a result, their subsequent actions could easily be 'sadly mistaken'. In just one case in the interviews, a review of goals and relationships was mentioned, and this was a written report to the bishop at the end of a curate's first year.

If regular monitoring of the curate's contract/job description were agreed, say every three to four months, there would be an expectation that different perspectives would be discussed between vicar and curate on an ongoing basis. Situations arising from different perspectives would then be much less likely to reach conflict or even crisis level, and later stages of a curacy could be more constructive.

In addition, the monitoring could be discussed as a matter of course at the annual appraisal with the bishop. This would avoid the hidden nature of many problems for curates, one of the factors of the Double Bind outlined in Chapter 11. Putting it in the framework of regular assessment by the vicar or the bishop would also prevent the risk of curates seeming to have a complaint, if initiation of difficulties or differences is left to them. A review or appraisal has more bite if there is a clear written job description to act as some sort of benchmark.

The data from the interviews suggested that when difficulties arose the main support for the curate usually came from his wife. If difficulties reached a point of conflict, this seemed to be dealt with through individual interviews with the bishop rather than the vicar and curate together meeting with him, or with someone appointed to work with the differences. If resolution or new understanding can be brought about through monitoring, as the Psychological Contract suggests, vicar and curate need not be left with a sense of blame or failure and the clergy family can be set free from a role which belongs elsewhere.

4. Changes and life stages

One couple's story illustrates the extra problem if the diocese should hit a life-cycle stage at the same time that a curate's family needs support or advice. They thought they had a fairly realistic expectation of a curacy and in fact found it better than they had anticipated. The vicar had been straight with them when they asked probing questions without making out that 'it was all hunky dory'. He had been an easy person to work with.

But that vicar moved after 18 months and the curate had an interregnum to handle during which his father died. He found the relationship with the new vicar particularly stressful. His wife was finishing a university course so they could not just move. He said that, looking back, if he had had support from the diocese to help with the relationship or to find another parish nearby it would have made a great deal of difference. 'At the time, though, the diocesan bishop was seriously ill, one archdeacon was ill, the other about to leave, and the suffragen bishop was covering his own and three other people's jobs. The whole diocese was in absolute chaos.' His wife said that they had not realized until they moved to their present diocese how the experience had drained them. In the midst of 'the chaos', no one had noticed the couple's own very real needs.

Two other families also found themselves with a change of vicar. In secular employment, situations can change very quickly but the difference for clergy is the particular intensity of the vicar/curate relationship and the all-enveloping nature of the job.

5. The Reference Groups' comments and the Generational Divide

This was the first time that the Pastoral Group mentioned a generational divide. They felt that some older clergy who were training vicars might work within a paternalistic framework and, as in previous generations, curacies would be seen by this older generation as halcyon days, with all responsibility carried by the vicar. Until recently, most curates only had job descriptions rather than contracts and these might not be clear about expectations of the curate's role or who would carry responsibility.

The Leadership Group were surprised that so many newly-ordained priests had bad experiences in curacies and asked if this was due to poor training or the work itself. They thought more initial preparation for curacies was needed. They also felt that dioceses were not infallible in appointing and training the training vicars.

This Group thought curates had 'an initial "honeymoon period" until difficulties arose, although this could be two weeks, six months and not more than a year'. They felt that less-committed wives were then more likely to ask the bishop what *he* was going to do about it. They commented that it was difficult to recruit 'such couples' to 'tougher parishes'. Couples from an evangelical or charismatic background were seen to be more adaptable.

The Group were speaking of their experience generally and it was not clear if the lack of other channels for dealing with overall difficulties meant *spouses* were the ones who would approach the bishop. Had they attempted to solve the problems themselves at local or diocesan level but not received a response? If they went to the bishop as a last resort, would it mean that 'such couples' might give a negative impression and automatically be seen as less adaptable? The data suggested that the leadership did not have regular contact with clergy families so it was unclear how spouses' commitment would be assessed. The anxiety that they might give a negative impression might explain why curates seemed reluctant to contact the bishop even if they had no other source of support or direction.

Like the Pastoral Group, the Leadership Group spoke of hierarchical attitudes leading to complaints against vicars, but also said that some of the turmoil experienced by curates was 'the pain of professional apprenticeship as even senior men are junior curates when first ordained'. This again could indicate a generational divide. From the families' comments, they knew that significant training was necessary but had also anticipated that parishes would value and respect both the Christian and secular experience of the many older ordinands now becoming priests. Supervision and the sort of monitoring advocated in the Psychological Contract above, both of which are part of management structures in other caring professions, were not discussed.

II. PRESSURE TO CONFORM

1. A public identity

The children, as clergy children now, had a sense of being known, watched and labelled by both church members and the public. Younger children said they disliked their father wearing his dog collar when they were with him, as they felt conspicuous. Teenagers, sensitive at the best of times, were seeking to establish their own identity. Some had known family life before ordination. They found it very difficult now to be stereotyped and at times reacted with intense annoyance and a desire to shock, but were aware how this might affect their parent's job.

A daughter of 14 said her father was very popular, everyone in the community knew him and recognized her surname, so she couldn't be herself. 'You have an image to live up to. It's even more annoying that it's not his fault so I can't blame him.' At other times, she felt different but unknown as contemporaries knew her father was a curate but might not know what this meant. One boy at school said to her, 'A curate's someone who works in a garage, isn't he?'

Her 13-year-old sister felt that this image as clergy children was there before they even arrived, an image of being thoroughly boring, plain and uninteresting, and they were labelled before people got to know them. One day she refused an invitation. 'Because you're a vicar's daughter you won't go out with anyone'. She found people expected her to be a Christian because her 'father was a vicar'. 'I think that's wrong. I have to make that choice myself.'

A 16-year-old spoke very strongly. 'When people have the sort of attitude, "Oh, you're the curate's son" with a feeling that you're supposed to be of a certain status and meeting certain standards, I'd dearly love to show their teeth my fist. I don't because I'm too restrained.' His older brother said that he never mentioned who his parents were if people didn't know.

Parents agreed with their children's view of a clergy family image. A father said he had noticed 'a guardedness' towards his children from their contemporaries, a situation he could compare with the family's pre-ordination experience. A mother, also aware of the image, said, 'We do row. I don't think there is a family that doesn't – as probably our neighbours can hear, unfortunately.' In their discussion the Pastoral Group recognized that clergy children felt the father's status was high profile and wished he would not be noticed.

2. Twitching the net curtains and running to tell your mother

'I can't wait to get away from this parish', said a girl of 16. 'I'm really fed up. It's like living under a microscope. You feel you're watched at every corner and people are twitching net curtains whatever you do and reporting back. It's incredibly annoying and frustrating and makes you want to do stupid things just to give them something to run to your mother about'. In the previous interview she said that as brothers and sisters, she felt they stuck together, 'us, and them trying to wreck our lives; the parish intruding, gossiping about us. Sticking together makes us know that we are not the sole victim'. Her sister agreed and both felt they would get on better as a family if they were not living so close to both the church and the vicarage.

The children disliked having to baby-sit for younger siblings when parents were at services, or having to go to boring church events for other age groups. Nearly all the families had come from larger, lively churches and several parents commented that their present churches were not easy for young people, with little going on for them. Three older teenagers from different families decided to go to more lively churches where they had a sense of 'being their own person'. None of this changed the expectations of their involvement from parishioners such as answering the telephone at all hours, knowing what was going on in the parish and being willing to get 'roped in' to do odd jobs.

A mother who had been a clergy daughter herself was very aware of the dangers. Her husband recalled the games her mother had played: 'Daddy would be very disappointed if you were not there' or 'You've got to do it otherwise people will think badly of Daddy'. She wanted her children to be free to choose what they did in church. Another family protected their children from church functions because their vicar and his wife were at everything, and they stopped trying to keep up.

A great deal of pain, anger and helplessness was expressed by the young people at the imposed public image and because they were known and watched. Expectations, whether stated or hinted at, could cause strong personal reactions. They found a variety of ways of combating the problems but were usually mindful of comeback on the family of any actions they might take.

III. LOSS OF PERSONAL IDENTITY

1. Loss of status

A wife and son had both spoken of the loss of status for the priest after nearly 20 years as a highly qualified research engineer in industry, heading a research department. His son thought he missed being his own boss and missed his friends at work because they were 'all doing the same things together'. The husband said there had been a loss of status for his wife too. She said that she missed her specialist teaching and consultancy work. As a theological student's wife she had been 'behind him' much more, whereas previously she had been very much her own person. They knew he would be the 'up front person' but she felt it was something they were being called to do together.

For the families, the focus of their comments had been the loss of identity faced by the whole family in relation to the ordinand's change from a previous career to becoming a student and then a curate. This had been a very significant experience, especially for ordinands and their wives who had had careers for a considerable time beforehand.

2. The Reference Groups' comments

When we discussed with the Groups the loss of status for the families with the many changes they faced, they initially passed it over almost without comment.

The Pastoral Group felt that the ordination process itself associates people with social status, and this status would be lost if priests left the ordained ministry and returned to secular life. They also thought this was one reason why clergy would be more likely to stay if they had a mid-life crisis or loss of faith. They felt ordination implied having charisma and social skills, so those more introverted and less 'good with people' would have status but be seen 'not to be delivering the goods'.

They thought parishioners often put priests above criticism because of their status, even elevating them in the pulpit. There could then be a discrepancy between the families' experience of them and the public image. The family would be aware of the hypocrisy but could get caught up in a pretence that they lived up to this image. The Group asked what the priests then did with, say, their aggression and sexuality. Did the aggression, for example, go back into the family? There was also discussion about clergy changing in response to public expectations, such as developing an intoning clerical voice, and spouses being God's gift to keep them normal.

Members of the Leadership Group saw the effect of ordination from another point of view. For them, loss of status was necessary for curates as their previous secular profession would only be of value at the next stage of ministry. First they needed to go through 'the dark night of the soul',[2] helped by colleagues, the diocese, post-ordination training chaired by a senior cleric, or their support group. The Group said clergy were now marginalized in society – a loss of magic. A curate would be told by his vicar, 'we are nobodies'. Accepting this could bring liberation. The Group also spoke of 'becoming low status', 'the priest with his people'. They did not mention how the family would be involved in all of this process.

The Group asked several questions about clergy wives. Were they in sympathy with their husband's vocation or were they 'jealous of God'? What were husbands' expectations of their wives? How should bishops react to wives who did not want to be regarded as clergy wives? Attention was on the husband in training, so she was an also-ran.

The Pastoral Group later commented, more in line with the families' meaning, that self-image and status are tied in with one's job, family and friends and there was need for the priest and the family to find a whole new self-image in the new context of ordination. This was also felt to be particularly difficult for young curates' partners 'having to act like someone more mature', leading to isolation and loneliness. Not all curates or even vicars' wives were confident or used to adapting to a range of situations. This comment was illustrated in the section on Moves in Chapter 7 by the curate's wife who spoke of moving to college as 'a move into nothingness'. 'Loss of status' had been the families' expression and we realized afterwards that perhaps speaking of 'loss of identity' or 'having to find a completely new self-image', rather than 'loss of status', would have helped the Reference Groups to look at the issue from a different angle.

It is interesting that the American Cornerstone Project[3] concluded that ministry had previously been high status and low stress, but had now become low status and high stress. Chapters 13–18, giving the data from the families at the incumbency stage as they took on more responsibility, will add to this debate.

---

2   The Oxford Dictionary of Quotations says, 'The phrase "dark night of the soul" was used as the Spanish title of a work by St. John of the Cross known in English as *The Ascent of Mount Carmel* (1578–80)'. The Dictionary also refers to F. Scott Fitzgerald (1896–1940) who wrote in *The Crack-Up* 'In the real dark night of the soul it is always three o'clock in the morning'.

3   Episcopal Church Foundation and The Alban Institute (1989) *The Cornerstone Project: Personal and Professional Development of the Clergy of the Episcopal Church.* New York: The Episcopal Church Foundation.

IV. COURTSHIP AND MARRIAGE

1. Job or marriage first?

Comments of two families suggested that the difficulties of a courtship in the public eye could be a particular factor in the decision of couples to get married when they did. For one man the reality of the public aspect was shown when the parish in which he was a curate, including the rector, wanted the couple to be married in that parish rather than in the bride's home church. Only four members of the parish had accepted their invitation to the wedding, although the couple had anticipated a coachload.

One couple were married at the end of his training. She had been ill for the previous year so still had to complete the final year of her teaching degree. They had been engaged for two years so they did not want to postpone their wedding. Rather than looking for a parish near her course, his college Principal persuaded him to return to his home, sponsoring diocese, which was some distance away. He felt they did not settle down as a married couple until the end of their first year. During that time they were together only for weekends and holidays. He did not mention whether or not the Principal had discussed the situation with his bishop or Diocesan Director of Ordinands. He described the whole situation as being 'cruelly ill-advised and even cruelly encouraged by people who should have known better'.

The sense was that the job had to come before the needs of the couple. But was this inevitable? To what extent would it have been appropriate for him to raise personal issues at this early stage or to ask about his commitment to his sponsoring diocese in these unexpected circumstances? With whom could he have discussed the dilemma? If he had talked to his Diocesan Director of Ordinands or approached his Bishop, would he resolve the problem but be seen as someone who would tend to buck the system before he was even in post? Would he then carry that label into the future? The Leadership Group's comments at the end of this chapter would suggest that this risk was real.

The man himself did not realize all the implications for them as a couple and did not reach the point of approaching the Bishop. What is surprising is that the college Principal, from experience, did not take the implications into account. Was he in fact also concerned about bucking the system? For curates the extent or flexibility of the system is quite unknown.

One couple spoke of their experience some years before. They re-met during her nursing training. They were engaged after a few weeks and married ten months later. She was 21. She did not finish her full training: 'The bishop was really fantastic about that, saying, "Of course it's more important to get married". The nurse tutor was excellent and understood, too.'

For this couple there appeared to be no mention of the fact that her qualification might prove an invaluable asset when or if, at a later stage, she needed a job to augment her husband's stipend. She did try to finish her training at a nearby hospital after their marriage, but the system of continuous assessment made a transfer impossible. It would have been interesting to know whether their Bishop's wife had had her own career, in view of Jolly's comment[4] that Army officers tended to recommend solutions to problems that they had used themselves.

One wife with a demanding executive job had a complicated lengthy journey after their marriage. 'I had moved house, area, church and job all at once and was working elsewhere. I was unable to get involved with the church and all I was doing in the parish was sleeping.' Finally exhaustion and time off work made her take a less satisfactory job at a lower level nearer the new parish.

Several of the couples had been married one or two years before ordination. During his curacy the wives were finishing their professional training or working and having to negotiate moves and changes of job. One completed her ordination training but was unable to take up a paid post because there was insufficient time for her to complete a curacy before her husband was due to move.

2. The Reference Groups' comments

The Pastoral Group said that 20 or 30 years ago, curates were married in their second curacy or later, so were married first to the church. A wife might expect an absolute commitment from her husband to their marriage; he might feel a higher commitment to his job, leading to a lack of honesty. The congregation might see itself as a 'wife' in terms of expecting be put first, leading to rivalry, and making the curate seem like a bigamist. The conflict might not be obvious when the

---

4 Jolly, R. (1987) *Military Man, Family Man: Crown Property?* London: Brassey's Defence Publishers.

man was first ordained, but when conflict did arise, the Group felt that the parish always won. They linked it to the priest's guilt at taking time off and possibly self-generated expectations, and felt permission to take time off should not only be given, but emphasized, by bishops.

The Leadership Group commented that there were fantasies around a single curate making it difficult for him to get to know a prospective partner and there was an early expectation of seriousness in a relationship. 'Looser morals' of today meant higher expectation of clergy. Members of the Group asked, 'Should we dissuade couples from getting married and being ordained at the same time?'

The Pastoral Group commented that there was a vested interest in ignoring clergy marriage problems, presumably because they were breaking the ideal image. Difficulties, therefore, tended to be dealt with in terms of crisis. There needed to be more emphasis on ongoing support systems for clergy marriages, and support groups for clergy wives.

V.   DAYS OFF OR TIME AWAY FROM DAILY WORK

An additional dilemma for clergy families seemed to lie in parishioners' understanding of a 'day off'. The data suggested this was very far from free time. Clergy could be at meetings until 10–10.30 pm on the evening before. All family tasks and responsibilities as well as personal and family activities had to be concertina-ed into that 24 hours. If time ran out, the tasks might have to be taken over by their spouses. There were also very stringent financial restraints on outings to counteract the pressure, especially at the curacy stage.

It is interesting that the term 'leave' has spread from the Armed Services to holiday periods in many jobs. This now indicates not only 'on vacation' but also 'not at work' and gives a much clearer sense of a boundary between work and leisure. If clergy are involved in church activities on their day off, it is a continuation of their job and they are not 'on leave' from work issues. Consequently the boundary between work and leisure is denied.

Many parishioners voluntarily give much time to the church in a variety of ways when they are not at work, which can be very demanding. However, discussions in the interviews suggest that if parishioners see this as giving up their free time to the church/God/or even to the vicar personally, they see no reason why priests should not give up their free time too, even though for them it means returning to work.

Unless clergy are on leave on their day off there is no clear work/family boundary for their families either, especially as clergy are working from home. A further difficulty is that the Leadership Group's discussions showed that bishops and archdeacons struggle with this boundary as much as, if not more than, other clergy. It may then be difficult for them to emphasize a distinction that they find very hard to keep for themselves.

VI. EXPECTATIONS

For the families who took part in the research, the involvement of clergy wives in their husbands' jobs during his curacies has been seen in previous sections. They will share in the choice of parish and move with him to a specific place and house. Her career may be subordinate to his. Many of the issues faced by curates' wives over their own jobs were similar to those encountered by any wife who might move at the point of marriage or job change. The additional factor was adapting to a new public role and the extra commitment of involvement in the parish.

The couples had raised the issue of expectations of the wives' involvement at interview but like the husbands' job descriptions the initial clear picture did not always prove to be the same on the ground. She would almost certainly be expected to deal with callers while her husband was out. Parishioners may think she knows all that her husband has been told and will answer on his behalf, or act as a messenger. It took time and considerable concern for the couples to know the best way to address unreasonable expectations of wives and impositions they experienced. It might not be possible to address them at all because the exact source of those expectations or disapproval was not always clear.

Expectations of the part a wife would play in a parish seemed to depend on parish tradition and the age of the children. If previous curate's wives or the vicar's wife worked, there was less pressure for a clergy wife to be 'around in the parish'. One had waited to choose the jobs she wanted to do in the parish and had refused others, but then thought some people had been shocked when she said 'No' because they had traditionally been done by the curate's wife.

Another was given assurances that there would be no expectations of her but it was mentioned that she would receive an honorarium, 'part of the parish from the mists of time', for answering the phone and just being there. After several months, a churchwarden said she had not been 'doing the job', although the couple had no idea how this might have been judged. The couple refused the honorarium if there were particular undefined expectations attached. The situation was resolved and the honorarium paid, but the couple remained uncertain about overall expectations of her 'being around more in the church'.

Previous curates' wives had not worked outside parish life and she thought the churchwardens and others would have disapproved if they had known from the beginning that she anticipated working part-time. In the end, her husband had felt it necessary to mention in a sermon her work writing Bible commentaries, which was not apparent to many in the congregation.

The wives mentioned a range of involvement in church and voluntary activities, including teaching in Sunday School, and giving talks to groups such as Mothers' Unions. Some were co-running youth work and house groups, preparing and/or typing the parish magazine and leading the choir or playing the organ, even when the children were pre-school age. One had links with a women's refuge and had homeless people to meals. There was also organizing banner- and vestment-making.

VII. REFLECTIONS

These comments from the families and Reference Groups illustrate the many issues for the students and their families in choosing a curacy and living with that decision. Time restraints, the lack of clear job descriptions, few clear guidelines for teasing out different views of the job within a parish, and possible changes of vicar can make this a hazardous process with so many unknowns and individual agendas. These are in addition to the housing and education issues.

The chapter also highlights the divided loyalties of families between the job, the public image, expectations and the families' needs. Parishioners may expect curates to match any time that they give to helping in the parish in their 'time off'. They may not take into account that this is then a continuation of the curates' regular job, whereas for them it is a choice for their time away from their daily work. This may lead to unrealistic demands and confusion.

The teenagers in particular spoke very strongly about expectations of them in many aspects of their lives, both from church members and contemporaries. The 'unwritten contract' of the job for them, as well as their parents, could be very difficult to handle. The impression was that families felt they were negotiating a minefield.

9 The Cost

I. FINANCE

1. Funding for training

Before starting training, ordinands discuss the family's circumstances with their Diocesan Director of Ordinands (DDO) to decide their financial need and the level of help a diocese should give. The Train-a-Priest Fund (TAP Fund), set up in 1952 for the support of ordinands' families, now provides additional help to dioceses to meet this need.

In a leading article on 4 April 1996, when gifts to the TAP Fund since its inception reached £2 million, The *Church Times* wrote, 'Behind every gift there lies an appreciation of the financial sacrifices which men and women make when they enter the ordained ministry. Many things have changed since 1952, but this sacrifice from the ordinands and from their families has remained a constant feature of clergy training. Things are better now than they were when ordinands with families had to use their own savings or rely on the benevolence of trusts, or when individual dioceses had discretion over how much they needed to give. Even today, when ordinands' income is set at an arbitrary £2,700 below the stipend of a deacon, families can experience hardship'. At that stage the national average salary of a deacon, i.e. a curate in his probationary year, was £12,570 so, deducting the £2,700, on average, ordinands would receive help from dioceses to bring their annual income *from all sources* to £9,870. The average gross earnings before benefits in April 1996, for a family of two adults and 2.4 children, were £24,267 (Central Statistical Office). The average age of ordinands in 1993 was 37. Three of the four families in which the priest was still a curate at the start of our research had children who were or became teenagers during their father's curacy, so the financial pressure the families faced is self-evident. This dilemma has now been recognized, and although the pressure still remains, ordinands can apply to a hardship fund, set up under the umbrella of the TAP Fund.

One family with two children almost in their teens were left without financial advice because the Diocesan Director of Ordinands (DDO) was on the verge of retiring and said he could not help. Ordinands would have no idea how appropriate it would be to approach, say, the bishop instead. In fact this applicant wrote to the Advisory Board for Ministry for additional funding. The family paid for his second year of college themselves, getting into debt and having to pay the last term's fees out of the sale of their house.

Retrospectively his college principal wrote to the archdeacon in his home diocese. This resulted in a payment of £70, which was said to be as much as the diocese could afford. The family also received a small amount of help each term from their home church and said they were by no means the only people at college who faced this sort of problem. Their situation highlighted the potential impact of a life-cycle stage in the diocese, in this case the retirement of the DDO.

2.   Personal housing

Four families spoke of the different ways in which they had dealt with housing and the difficulties they had faced. One sold their house, bought one near college and sold again before he was ordained. They felt they could not buy again with the little capital that remained and could not afford to keep that house. They had invested the proceeds but 'of course it hasn't kept pace with inflation'.

Another family decided to sell their house and rent accommodation while he trained. A third couple attempted to sell but the housing market fell sharply, so they let it and rented a spare clergy house near college.

A wife with four children remained in their house. Life, she said, was very disjointed but even so the most difficult thing had been finance.

Their diocese worked on the principle of giving everybody money for basic necessities and the DDO said they were to go and see him with any major problems and 'we'll work something out'. On two occasions they had needed £500 and £600, one a bill for their ageing car. They found it very hard to ask for help. The husband felt the diocese was very supportive but his wife added, 'in a crisis, yes', but what constituted a crisis?

A vicar's family had sold their home when the husband was a curate. The wife had not worried too much because, coming from an

RAF family, she had lived in quarters, not her own home. She'd seldom worried about money but at times wondered what would happen on retirement. She thought it worried her husband more. Ruth Jolly[1] suggests that many more families of all ranks in the Armed Services now buy their own home rather than live in quarters. Clergy of course must live in the house provided.

3. The Reference Groups' comments

The Pastoral Group realized the financial pressure for clergy families, and felt they could barely live on the stipend alone. They also asked whether the families expected different standards to clergy in the past. They did not specifically link this question to their statement that they felt the Church of England still worked on the basis of clergy having private means.

One Group member said that families in difficulties 'needed a huge amount of help'; another mentioned clergy with previous careers 'dipping into their savings'. They also thought that the great variation in expenses between wealthy and poor parishes led to an unfair system.

The Leadership Group felt that few clergy families manage to reduce their lifestyle. They asked, 'Is the car or the credit card the reason for debt'? They considered that if a partner was not working then a £500 debt for car repairs, mentioned anxiously by the family above, was nothing; over £25,000 was a lot. Conversely, if the partner had a high salary there might be 'polarization within the couple'. They said that finance could be discussed with clergy at Post-Ordination Training but asked, 'How can bishops talk to clergy partners?' They thought that archdeacons or churchwardens could have a helpful relationship with the vicarage. The culture of an area or diocese should be that sharing problems would not 'merit a black mark'. They did not mention the crossing of the personal/work boundary that this type of 'helpful relationship' would involve. The availability of independent advice with professional consultants might feel much more appropriate to the families.

Their comments again suggested that the spouses' income was

1 Jolly, R. (1987) *Military Man, Family Man: Crown Property?* London: Brassey's Defence Publishers.

crucial to the families' ability to cope. The families' comments on lack of money for holidays and children's activities, and having to sell a caravan used for holidays and days off, all suggested they had already reduced their lifestyle considerably.

II. HEALTH

1. Health and previous history

Only one of the families still at the curacy stage or having recently moved to an incumbency reported illness. A wife had been diagnosed with rheumatoid arthritis after several weeks of concern. She had been confined for a month. Her husband felt her recovery had begun when they had their first proper holiday for ten years with three full weeks away. Their daughter said her mother's illness had affected her father too as he had had more to do in the family. On holiday there had been time for them all to relax. At the same stage the father had noticed a melanoma on his neck, which had been checked after six months and removed after a year.

This couple had been accepted for training eight months after having a baby who lived only a few days and following a traumatic death in the family some years earlier, which they talked about in the interviews. They began college nine months later, having sold their house albeit with complications, and with delays in renting a house in time and organizing schools for their children. After two more years they moved to a parish with all the attendant readjustments. They said that the parish, friends and the bishop all knew of her illness. Two things were not clear: one was who was aware of their previous history; the second was the question of whether a longer-term history for this family was sought during selection for ordination. This would have shown the complexity of their situation.

2. The Clergy Family Iceberg

To conduct the interviews we visited the families in their homes, so it was probably inevitable that there would be some conversation outside the interview proper, especially as we had often travelled long distances and would be offered tea or coffee while the family gathered. We have been meticulous about including only information shared during the interviews, or have given the source of other information relevant to the subject. However it seems important to record that we learnt from the parents in one family before the third interview that a teenager had overdosed between two of our visits.

In the interview the mother said that the teenager had been under a lot of pressure during the year with exams but she did not feel it would be fair to say more. The father commented that they had deliberately not planned what they were going to say or discussed it together, so they were not sure whether there were certain things that other members of the family wanted them to say or not. This family had been very open in previous interviews but the overdose was not spoken of during that session.

The family had experienced avoidable pressures during moves because of lack of parish co-ordination. The priest had worked very long hours with little support or encouragement and his wife had had additional training during the curacy. There had also been difficult educational issues for all three children related to moves, including this young person in question being left behind to complete earlier exams. The teenagers in this family had also expressed strongly how difficult they found it to live so much in the public eye with constant expectations from the parish for all of them. Other factors were almost certainly involved, but the overall situation of the family may well have contributed to such a severe reaction.

In the American Episcopal Families Network research[2] the assessors felt that statistics from other sources in the dioceses taking part indicated that problems had been under-reported. This incident raised the question to what extent serious issues for the families, especially ones of such a sensitive nature, had not been raised during the interviews, and how much of the clergy family iceberg was still hidden from public view even at this early stage of ministry.

III. THE CURATES' VIEW OF THE JOB

In 1993 the average age of ordinands was 37 compared with 32 in 1973. These statistics suggest not only that ordinands now are more likely to have children when they are ordained, but also indicate that

2   Episcopal Families Network (1988) *Episcopal Clergy Families in the '80s.* New York: The Episcopal Church Foundation.

ordinands would have significant previous employment experience with which to compare their experience in a curacy. In addition, they would have held positions of responsibility in their churches before ordination. This would have given them experience of the ecclesiastical system, although the Leadership Group had spoken of 'the pain of professional apprenticeship, as even senior men are junior curates when first ordained'.

Many of the issues that concerned the curates related to absence of boundaries, particularly in four areas: responsibility; communication; time management and the place of the family; and working from home.

1. Boundaries and responsibility

The clergy had commented that their interpretation of their job description had often been very different to that of the vicar, parish officials or members. The lack of structure, together with poor communication, led to them having little influence over the general shape of ministry in their parish. Often they were not given responsibility for specific areas of the work. They spoke of feeling excluded from decisions, not receiving general information and being given 'the odd jobs' or only part of a project to complete. There was an overall sense that their experience and capabilities were sidelined and under-used.

One man said he had ended up with 'quite a lot of responsibility to make sure things don't go wrong, and precious little authority to make sure they go right or go anywhere at all'. There was a sense in which the three years of his curacy had been terribly stultifying. 'I can't remember when I last actually got excited about possibilities in ministry because what is the point? Nobody is likely to follow through on anything I suggest. To be fair I think that's because there's a tremendous inertia in this particular parish.'

He had a good relationship with his first vicar but he moved after a year. The curate described the ensuing process. There had been no new initiatives in the months before the vicar left, then maintenance of the status quo by the team vicars during the interregnum, so that the new incumbent could introduce his own specific ideas. The new incumbent was cautious by nature, liked to keep a tight rein and found it difficult to delegate, so the sense of inertia and lack of responsibility that the curate felt continued over that extended period.

He thought he would continue to be frustrated until he had the privilege of taking responsibility for 'things that go right, carrying the can for things that go wrong, and being able to relate directly to church wardens and other leaders instead of indirectly as so often happens at the moment'.

Responsibility without support could be equally difficult. If one curate suggested something, his vicar would tell him to 'give it a good go'. The curate appreciated this, but it had created tensions when in various instances his new initiatives, such as starting an evening youth service, had been seen as 'the curate's thing'. The vicar had not owned them as clergy decisions so he felt very much alone and isolated in those situations.

Many of the curates had carried considerable responsibility in their secular jobs. One expressed a sense of satisfaction, in contrast to the general sense of frustration, in being given responsibility for organizing a mission for schools from beginning to end.

2. Boundaries and communication

Lack of feedback from the incumbent was a concern of several clergy at the curacy stage. One said that he never had feedback from his vicar. Another compared this with 17 years' experience in industry where 'you were always aware of overseeing and observing people's performance but there was always feedback built into it. It was a two-way thing, a regular system of appraisal'. He found it intensely frustrating that this was not happening. From a wider perspective, he said his peer group experience in a curacy was that this did not seem to be the pattern within the curate/training vicar relationship. 'No matter how many people write it down as part of the system, and the training incumbents are told how it should be, I find so few of them actually seem to do it'.

Negative but inexplicit feedback was also a problem. One curate felt he had not only lost autonomy in the area of work as a teacher, which he had for so many years, but was having to cope with a sense of constantly being devalued by his colleagues. They indicated that he was not competent but would not explain why, or discuss it openly, and this was one of the biggest pressures. The whole feeling of not being supported had been very difficult. He did not know how far it was a matter of very different styles within the team or something he needed to put right as well. Rather than saying that he did not work well as part of a team, he felt it was only as part of *that* team. However, without an opportunity to explore the difficulties in supervision or team consultancy he would probably carry the uncertainties into his first living.

Receiving encouraging feedback from the congregation had been very affirming to two curates who spoke of a growing confidence in preaching. Had the rector noticed? 'The thing is that having three churches he and I were in different places and he did not hear many of my sermons, so I don't know. We didn't talk about that sort of thing.'

Two other curates spoke of the growing sense of confidence that had come from the experience of running the parish, in one case after the vicar had moved and in the other during his vicar's three-month sabbatical. A few months before, one would not have wanted to move to greater responsibility, the other wondered how he would cope. Now they felt affirmed by things people had said and there was a sense of consolidation.

The appropriate level of feedback he should give to the PCC was a concern for one curate, who had always been very analytical, and wondered if people saw this as moaning. 'At one meeting when I felt perhaps I'd said too much, a PCC member said it was so refreshing to have a curate who had an opinion.'

3. Boundaries and time management – open all hours

A curate described his vicar as a clergyman of the old school who believed that you gave your all to the church and were always available. The vicar 'argued that he needed a full day off but seldom took it', so the parishioners wanted the curate to do things on his day off too. 'It's very difficult not to be dragged along in the vortex of someone who's a bit like the white tornado'.

The couple acknowledged that at first in his secular post he had been very keen to learn and get on and had worked extremely hard out of hours. In time he realized that you were probably more efficient if you had more time off rather than working so long and 'I think we've seen the same here'.

Another curate echoed his son's feeling that there was a lack of time for the family as he was out most evenings. They had to try to make quality time (a phrase often used by the families) of days off. He tried to have an hour's lunch break with his wife so in some ways 'we do better than people working away from home'. However, his sons were working or at school, so their main free time was in the evening. An Anglo-Catholic curate said his day began at 5.30 am. to allow time for personal prayer before mass at 6.30. He did a 70 or 80-hour week and did not see that he would have any more control over that when he had his own parish. Some days the family seemed to be completely squeezed out, which gave him a sense of guilt. 'They need a visit too!' He hoped they used the time together more advantageously as it became more valuable.

The picture was of a largely absent father. The verbal messages from the vicar and congregation were that family time was very important but in practice it became marginalized. This would be the pattern and the message that curates took into parishes of their own.

4. Boundaries and working from home

Most of the curates found it difficult to have their home and office together because of interruptions, especially to meals or days off. One said, 'It would be nice to lock the office and go home. Instead you are always at the office because it is there'.

Another commented that this was his second experience of having an office at home. 'It is interesting that each time my office has been untidy at home but not in the work place. I find it fascinating. I haven't worked out why'. His comment emphasized the whole question of boundaries. If one could never close the door on work, when was it finished? And, as we asked an eight-year-old daughter, when did it begin? She had replied so graphically, 'As soon as he opens his eyes'.

IV. REFLECTIONS

It seemed that curates and their families were committed to upholding the ideal of the job and therefore accepted their situation, especially at this early stage of ministry. This could mean that they did not speak of financial pressures or even 'crises' unless these were critical. They might go on attempting to continue with commitments until an illness or problem became severe enough to give them no option but to stop. Even very serious problems such as the attempted suicide mentioned above might remain hidden from the hierarchy, parishioners and possibly wider family. The varied messages about family time from all sources and the role model of the hierarchy said very clearly that the job must come first.

Overall, the clergy in the research found it difficult to work within 'somebody else's organizational framework' when there were no clear structures, few if any areas of responsibility, no system of appraisal between vicar and curate, and little or no regular feedback. Any recorded encouragement came from members of congregations rather than within the curate/training vicar relationship. There seemed to be various areas that were just not talked about, whether these concerned possible deficiencies that needed to be addressed, or important evaluation that was not made, such as review of sermons. Responsibility for the parish during sabbaticals or an interregnum made the prospect of more responsibility in their next job much less daunting.

Guidelines given to training vicars seemed largely to be ignored, and one curate said this had also been the experience of all his college contemporaries, suggesting the difficulty could be widespread. There was no regular supervision for vicars and their curates together to examine differences, strengths and goals. This again is interesting when compared with the regular reviews mentioned within the Psychological Contract discussed in Chapter 8, I. 3. The Pastoral Group in their discussion said a counsellor outside the hierarchy could help to clarify 'fudged boundaries' but as this would be personally focused, it would not necessarily be a substitute for regular supervision and appraisal in a professional context.

The question may be whether the Church is prepared to use its personnel to the full or to allow them to become demoralized and lacking in confidence because training issues are given a low priority by training vicars. In a letter to The *Church Times* on 24 May 1996, the Bishop of Hull said how important he considered it to encourage 'young men and women of calibre with the right gifts and experience to offer for ordained ministry', including second career priests, 'to serve the Church as leaders'. If the 'men of calibre' in the research, with a significant and successful first career behind them, were treated with so little sense of value and respect as people, one of the Churches' greatest resources may be being squandered.

10 Reflections on Issues at the Curacy Stage

I. DILEMMAS

As well as summarizing the family interviews for discussion by both Groups, we sent an additional summary to the Leadership Group. This highlighted three dilemmas for the families that had been particularly noted by the Pastoral Group in their meeting. These were: control; leadership and dependency; and the separation of discipline and pastoral care. The Pastoral Group felt that underlying all these dilemmas was a need for honesty: at the personal level; between husband and wife; within the family; and in the hierarchy. There was a strong feeling that issues were dealt with too late. Under each dilemma, the Pastoral Group's comments are summarized first, then the Leadership Group's response.

1. Control

We saw in Chapter 5 that at least some sense of control is fundamental to dealing with stress successfully. The Pastoral Group was struck by the evident lack of control the families had over many issues that they faced at this stage. The families assumed the bishop did have control so expected support and action to address the issues. Otherwise the resulting stress was taken into the heart of the family.

In response the Leadership Group challenged the assumptions about the nature of authority in a diocese. 'The reality is that nobody is in control or has single authority, that's the way it is, and bishops grumble and are frustrated by this most. The bishop cannot pull a lever and solve problems'. This issue was put back to the clergy saying that wanting to be dependent but liking control was the human battle in each of us. The Group also felt there was a lack of information to clergy about what was or was not possible.

2. Leadership and dependency

The Pastoral Group felt that the contradiction between being in a leadership role as clergy and being dependent on the parish for such important issues as housing, expenses, and decisions surrounding curacies, caused conflicting expectations at all levels. The Group felt this could undermine emotional support for the family from within the parish, especially in rural, new estate and urban priority areas, and could lead to their isolation.

The Leadership Group discussed the nature of leadership and whether the image was that of 'running the show'. They asked, 'Were clergy dependent for expenses or emotionally dependent?' because it seemed there was 'an assumption that everyone is required to be supported by everybody else'. They suggested that this was a male/female issue and things were 'coming into more of a female understanding'.

They spoke of there being no clear consensus of what the job is or whether guidance should come from above or from peers. So as the clergyman 'does not want to be idle, he does crazy things'. Students were seen to 'lack the ability to do anything for themselves'. The wife was spoken of as 'the expert', presumably about a problem in hand, and one member said that he would appreciate her 'giving the Diocesan Secretary an earful rather than weeping to the bishop'. This was more likely anyway to 'get action'.

3. Separation of discipline and pastoral care

Several couples spoke of the bishop as their Father in God and protector, but in a number of instances had been anxious about taking problems to him. The Pastoral Group advocated care of clergy with problems being separated from bishops and dealt with by counsellors.

The Leadership Group felt the issue was related to the bishop also being responsible for a man's job prospects. A bishop with a warm personality raised expectations of the result, but one who stands back might be more realistic and more effective. They felt the bishop and his staff were aware of wider issues, with the rural dean, counsellors and 'soul friends' each having a role.

They felt there was an assumption that once a bishop formally took office he would always be available and this gave wrong messages. A distinction between availability and accessibility was important.

Bishops' diaries were full but they would respond to emergencies with, 'Come at once if it's urgent, or in . . . weeks' which might be 6–12 weeks time. They said there needed to be communication about what additional support was available. Above all the bishop could not undermine the legitimate authority of other people.

II. REFLECTIONS ON THE FIRST REFERENCE GROUP MEETINGS

1. Comment on the Pastoral Group's response and concerns

The Pastoral Group showed considerable sensitivity to the families' position in the early stages of ministry. They were aware of a range of difficulties arising from: concerns about curates' housing; low stipend; the significant change of identity for all family members in becoming a clergy family; rivalry for the wife or children with the job; the public profile for both children and parents; and crisis management for clergy marriages in difficulties.

The Group's comments suggested that the whole context of ministry was affected by expectations at all different levels, from the parish, the diocese and the general public and these expectations meant considerations of the job came first before the family's needs and interests. The Group spoke of selecting a curacy as an all-enveloping situation and saw the difficulty of 'choosing your whole life in one day'. They thought that when ordinands went to see a parish it was important for them to state the family's needs clearly. The data showed that the families had in fact made very clear requests and tried to make appropriate decisions for themselves as the Group recommended, but had met with spoken and unspoken messages indicating little understanding of their position.

Although they saw the difficulties, the Pastoral Group did not indicate what action the families might take if their needs were ignored or considered invalid, or the parish had other agendas. They commented that with a three- or four-year curacy 'the end is in sight, therefore the family can accept it', and then discussed 'people's ability to adapt'. They did not comment, however, on the concern of both Reference Groups that if 'clergy were anxious to protect their public image as a Christian', their anger, aggression or frustration might be unloaded onto the family. If this happened over the period of a curacy and the family 'accepted it', the potential damage could be considerable and provoke a severe cycle of stress.

This hidden nature of many difficulties faced by the families was first highlighted in this round of interviews. Even if these were explored in counselling, bishops and other leaders might not know of the range of problems clergy families were facing, and so could not pre-empt or address them. The Pastoral Group suggested that it was also hard to know when problems concerned only the priest or family and when they spilled over into issues of concern for the bishop as line manager.

Counselling's code of confidentiality meant counsellors could only encourage clergy or family members to talk to the bishop, if this seemed appropriate. They were not free to report their own anxieties, however serious, unless there was risk to others or danger of self-harm. Both Groups felt there should be clear male/female boundaries as clergy were vulnerable to being over-idealized and set on a pedestal by parishioners. This might also make it harder for parishioners or others to know when this boundary had been crossed and to report concerns.

The Leadership Group suggested that if there was scandal, the bishop needed to know the issues to protect people, and the press expected him to know as 'only the bishop will do'. Supervision was essential if clergy undertook to counsel others. The whole discussion suggested that safeguards like supervision, which might be built into other organizational situations, could be ignored or confused. This was not only because of confidentiality but also the potential fantasy surrounding the image of a priest.

The Pastoral Group thought honesty was essential from the start between the couple. Work could be used as an excuse when there were marriage problems.

The Pastoral Group's own concerns about clergy family stress, which each Group had been asked to note before our first meeting with them, again centred round the overall themes of boundaries and expectations. The need for boundaries provided by clear job descriptions and effective management were emphasized in their comment that 'half of what a priest does is not what priests are ordained for'. Several other management issues were touched on: a need for strong emphasis by bishops for clergy to take appropriate time off; the importance of affirmation; protection from violence; the problem of isolation; and support rather than crisis management for clergy marriages.

The Group felt that self-denial and the servant image were at the heart of the Christian faith and were concerned that a priest might carry a sense of guilt if his family did not share these ideals in terms of commitment to the church and a denial of 'wealth'. Priests might also justify lack of time with the family on spiritual grounds. The Group felt that ordination still implied status and an expectation of a charismatic, outgoing personality, and suggested that 'a quieter person might be seen as not delivering the goods'. They did not say how these seemingly contradictory images might be addressed.

Discussion in each of these areas centred around the priest's ability to handle any associated problems. Thus the onus of dealing with the difficulties was left almost entirely with the families rather than responsibility for change and appropriate support also being held by the organization of the Church at each level.

2. Comment on the Leadership Group's response and concerns

The Leadership Group's comments suggested that dilemmas experienced by clergy and their families paralleled many of those faced by those in positions of leadership. There were the frustrations of a fragmented organizational system, which the Group expressed so strongly for themselves. There was uncertainty about the nature of authority and lack of clarity about who carried responsibility in different contexts. They considered that the nature of the clergy task was undefined. They spelt out the need for a distinction between availability and accessibility, which they saw as creating unrealistic demands, and talked of the intense pressure they experienced in the job.

They spoke with considerable openness and clarity about their own dilemmas, but they did not seem to see these dilemmas for clergy within the same framework, even though these had such impact on the families. Among their own concerns, which they were asked to note before the meeting, the Leadership Group mentioned a number of issues highlighted by both the families and the Pastoral Group. These included: problems of adequate curates' housing; pressure for children in inner-city schools; conflict caused by hierarchical attitudes of vicars towards curates; concern over stress and lack of stimulation; the public aspect of the role; the family living in a 'goldfish bowl' with idealistic expectations; and the need for care of clergy and their families by laity.

In most instances, they did not discuss possible solutions or more specific support to address these difficulties. They said that lack of information left clergy not knowing what to do but expecting the leadership to know and to have authority. The Group's perception was that in fact no one had authority. They did not suggest clear systems for communicating who did hold responsibility for particular issues, or how clergy could access help. Instead, they turned the situation back on the clergy, saying that the 'human battle in each of us is wanting to be dependent but have control'. They also moved on immediately from practical dependence over issues of housing, to emotional dependence, and 'everyone thinking they must be supported by everyone else' implying a lack of self-sufficiency.

The Group spoke of there being no clear consensus on the nature of the job or whether guidance should come from the hierarchy or from peers. Again the link was to the priest 'not wanting to be idle so he does crazy things' rather than to clarification and proper professional supervision. If those in positions of leadership were unclear, it would seem certain that clergy would be as well.

They emphasized the importance of good clergy/laity relationships, seen in a pattern of 'delegation, sharing and openness'. The data showed that this was not necessarily a model clergy received from the hierarchy, even on the brief occasions when they met. If clergy had problems the bishops thought it was best to be able to stand back and be realistic as 'a warm approach' could raise expectations of the result.

This suggested a move to a more professional approach, with bishops using their 'wider awareness' to guide clergy within clearer, professional boundaries. They did not spell out how this new approach might be communicated to clergy to clarify expectations. Apart from recourse to counsellors, there was very little other support mentioned by the families. They might receive much love and care from individual members of parishes but this did not address the practical issues that caused such concern. The wider networks of rural dean and 'soul friends', which the Leadership Group suggested were available to clergy, did not seem to offer effective or consistent support. Similarly the data did not indicate a sense of clergy being helped during 'the dark night of the soul' by 'colleagues, the diocese, post-ordination training, or their support group'. If the leadership thought these patterns of support were significantly available to clergy, they might not see the importance of setting up other systems.

The Group said there needed to be a distinction between bishops being accessible and being available. The interviews showed that clergy were very conscious of pressure on bishops' time and their perception was that the bishop was not automatically available. This could lead to clergy waiting till a situation was serious before approaching him, for instance the crisis management of marriages spoken of by the Pastoral Group. The clergy might not want the polarization of issues into a crisis category, 'come right now' or a low priority, 'come in 6–12 weeks'. Delay in being able to see a bishop would vary from diocese to diocese, but it seemed that often this pressure on bishops and clergy alike could be avoided if other channels of help for particular issues were made clear. The Group wanted a culture of problems being able to be shared without it entailing a black mark for clergy, but did not say how this cultural message might be passed through the organizational network.

Yet another pattern was that the Group thought clergy showed 'a well buried desire to succeed' and partners too may have thought they had married a high-flier. They did not indicate how this buried desire was shown. They said there needed to be a 'theology of failure or perceived failure'. The data, in fact, suggested a strong pragmatic desire by both clergy and clergy spouses to use their skills and abilities to the full where these were appropriate in the situation. When these were sidelined in curacies or dampened down for incumbents, there was marked frustration.

Any 'poison of disappointment', at whichever level, seemed to be linked by the clergy and families to lack of both contact with the hierarchy and of affirmation. This led to great uncertainty for clergy about whether their abilities were known and acknowledged within the system, so that their skills could be channelled appropriately. The Group did not suggest that any 'disappointment' in an organization with such a flat structure should be addressed at each stage of ministry through adequate professional consultation.

Equally, if clergy felt affirmed in their current situations, they would presumably be less likely to feel that they had failed. If situations were polarized into success or failure by the leadership they would also appear in this light to clergy, whereas different types of 'success' could be considered. In fact, success and failure in these contrasting terms were hardly mentioned by the families during the whole research. Their concern was to have an opportunity to discuss whether or not their approach and actions were of maximum benefit to the growth of the parish and to consider future directions. This type of discussion tended to happen only during annual appraisals not on a regular basis in supervision.

The greatest uncertainty for the Leadership Group seemed to centre round how to discuss financial, sexual, emotional or practical issues with clergy spouses, and how to deal with those who did not want to be identified in the role of clergy partners. The interviews suggested that these issues were equally uncertain for the spouses too, and indeed for all family members. No new systems of communication were suggested so that each side could hear the others' dilemmas within a framework of openness in which 'sharing problems would not merit a black mark', as the Group advocated. This left the families feeling exposed and unsupported.

At the end of the session the Group raised several issues for discussion in future meetings. These included having more bishops, which could mean a more reasonable workload for each individual bishop. A second issue was selection procedures generally and the use of family trees in those procedures. The relevance and value of these as a tool to give background information during selection were discussed in *Holy Matrimony*.[1] The final point was a reassessment of the six-day week for clergy.

It was striking that the Group framed many of the issues in black and white terms and placed responsibility firmly back onto the clergy or families. They only touched on whether questions should be asked about management systems. The number of questions that Group members asked throughout the session indicated a considerable degree of uncertainty about how to address the whole complex question of clergy family stress. This linked back to the early comments by two members of the Group that they were participating in the research to learn as well as to contribute.

Overall the information from the first round of interviews and the Group meetings showed that it was the families who were seen as unable to be independent, rather than the structures, which could make them independent, often being unclear and uncertain.

---

1 Kirk and Leary (1993) *Holy Matrimony? An Exploration of Marriage and Ministry.* Oxford: Lynx.

PART FOUR
A Pause for Thought

11 The Double Bind and the Accommodation Syndrome

I. THE DOUBLE BIND

After the first round of interviews we looked at different established ideas and theories that could help us to understand what the families and Reference Groups had said. We were then able to look at these ideas again after the second and third interviews to see further ways in which they might apply. We shall outline the ideas first, and suggest how they may be linked together at the end of Chapter 12.

Just after we started thinking about how ideas of the Double Bind might apply to clergy families, a friend telephoned and said how worried she and her husband were about their vicar and his wife. They had talked to us before about tensions in the parish and their concerns. Now it seemed that these had come to a head.

> 'What seems ridiculous is that they went completely over the top about something so insignificant. It happened at the end of our flower festival and suddenly they lashed out at a small group of us about tables in the church hall. We were all pretty tired but everyone who came thought it was so special and we'd worked together so well that we felt really encouraged. This just cast a shadow over everything.'

We said that from what she had described then and previously, it seemed there had been a lot of conflicting messages going back and forth between the vicar and his wife, and senior lay people who had tried to discuss some of their concerns. If, as a result, the couple had felt criticised or misunderstood or thought parishioners were unwilling to cooperate with their approach, they may have felt helpless or angry. It seemed that they had not been able to find the right way to express this or resolve the conflict.

We told her we had been trying to understand exactly these kinds of incident, which seemed out of all proportion to the immediate situation. We ran briefly through Bateson's[1] ideas of the Double Bind. We suggested that this couple may have been experiencing life in the parish as a double bind over many months or even years, and this unexpected outburst may have been the reaction of panic or rage that Bateson outlined. Our friend felt this threw new light on what had happened if the reaction was to the whole situation and not just to this incident.

1. Bateson's theory of the Double Bind

The Double Bind has echoes of a Catch 22 where either of two alternatives has a difficult or seemingly impossible outcome in the eyes of the person making the choice. In contrast, Bateson spelt out six specific elements to the Double Bind which must all be present for the Bind to apply. We shall outline these first and then link them to what the families said.

1. One or more people in authority impose the situation on the person or people concerned.
2. It is a repeated experience rather than a single, traumatic event, so they constantly expect the Bind to happen.
3. First, the people experiencing the Bind are given a negative command, which carries the threat of punishment, or other serious consequences implying that they would be to blame. An important point is that those in authority express helplessness to act in any other way. For instance they may say, 'You must do this particular thing, otherwise key people have said they will leave', or 'If you don't do this, the whole project will collapse'.
4. A secondary command is given which conflicts with the first but again is enforced by the threat or veiled threat of punishment. This secondary injunction may be given in a number of ways and is not always expressed verbally, for instance it may be highlighted by reactions, even a look of warning.

---

1 Bateson, G. (1972) *Steps to an Ecology of Mind*. New York, Ballantine Books.

5. There is then a third negative command prohibiting the victim from leaving or escaping from the field. Sometimes these commands are not purely negative but have the same impact as negative ones.
6. Once the subjects of the Bind have learned to view life in patterns of the Double Bind any part of the sequence may provoke panic or rage. This is the fourth factor.

Bateson mentioned two other factors:

1. One is that the victim of the Bind, usually because of their age or being in a dependent position, is unable to comment on the conflicting nature of the different messages.
2. The other is that the situation is made worse if there is no independent figure to intervene in the relationship between the two parties. In a family this might be a strong and insightful father or mother; in another situation it could be someone who has a different authority.

Bateson says that a Double Bind may apply in other situations than families.

2. Clergy families and expectations

One of the main difficulties for our research families was dealing with the many expectations, often contradictory, from a very wide range of people. This led us to consider how Bateson's ideas might apply specifically to them.

Bateson speaks of 'two or more persons'. If one party is the clergy family, the other party imposing the Bind may be one of several people or groups, including the bishop, the archdeacon, the church congregation or the communities in which the families live.

Although clergy families may experience certain traumatic moments, it is the long-term, cumulative effect of 'the repeated experience' that makes them anticipate the Double Bind.

At the ordination service clergy are required to promise to 'Strive to fashion your own life, and that of your household according to the way of Christ'. This is a positive injunction but it also implies 'do not do anything to break the ideal of this promise or this may have a damaging influence on your ministry. You will be letting God and the family down, the church family and your own'. So this can be seen as the main 'negative command' in terms of the Double Bind.

The families' comments showed that as Christians they would be keen for their family lives to reflect this promise, as well as it being expected of them by the different groups. Friedman's book on family process in churches and synagogues[2] highlights the expectation that the minister and his family should be all things to all people, non-judgmental, understanding and forgiving even if other members of the congregation fail to meet that ideal.

What became increasingly significant in the first interviews was the second command, implied or directly given to the families by all levels of the church and community, that 'the job must come first'. In this case the priest could not fulfil both injunctions. It would not be possible to 'fashion his household according to the way of Christ' with the love, attention and encouragement that this would imply if the job always had a prior claim. So this injunction would conflict with the first.

Although it would not be impossible for the clergy family to leave the field, it would be very difficult in several ways. The 'injunction' is that they are required to live in the house provided as a condition of the job. The families' comments showed that after selling their own house, if they had one, they would not have enough money to cover a mortgage on another house of their own. If they left, accommodation would then be a major difficulty.

Above all, the families' deep sense of commitment was expressed in many ways. Leaving would bring a sense of guilt for the priest and his family, as well as a sense of failed vocation both for the priest and the church as a whole. The clergy also spoke of the many changes in the field of their previous jobs in a fast moving technological age. One man had tried to get a temporary summer job as an engineer at theological college and was told he was already out of date in his field. He added, 'So this is what I can do and all I can do'. The third injunction, not to leave the field, had a strong reality for the families as the data from the third interviews clearly shows.

Bateson said that 'the complete set of ingredients is no longer necessary' as once the victim has learned to view life in patterns of the Double Bind, any part of the sequence could provoke panic or rage. The very strong reaction of clergy families, sometimes to a minor

2   Friedman, E.H. (1985) *Generation to Generation: Family process in church and synagogue.* New York, Guilford Press.

incident as in the example at the beginning of this chapter, fitted with this idea.

Certainly the older clergy children spoke of how they would sometimes have an urge to shock or lash out at people who criticised them or seemed to be watching them or had unreal expectations. Material from the two Reference Groups suggested that panic and rage might be expressed through inappropriate behaviour in financial, sexual or other contexts.

The 'inability to comment' and the 'lack of an intervening figure' from Bateson's thesis seem particularly applicable to clergy families. This is illustrated in the example given in section II.1 below. The Double Bind therefore seemed to fit with clergy families' experience and would be put alongside further information.

II. THE ACCOMMODATION SYNDROME

Clergy families had to cope with the different Double Binds they faced, sometimes over a period of months or years, and we were aware that a theory of the Accommodation Syndrome had been developed in various contexts. We explored how clergy families, caught in the Double Bind, might respond by 'accommodating' to the situation. It may seem confusing to be speaking of accommodation in another context when we have been discussing it in relation to housing but it is important to note the distinction here.

The Accommodation Syndrome relates to accepting or adapting to circumstances, however difficult they may be, because of the greater cost of speaking out or trying to change the situation. The principles of accommodation are spelt out particularly clearly by Summit.[3] He is referring to a situation within the system of a family. One of the most frequent images used by all involved in the research was of the Church as a family whether at local or diocesan level. His thesis can apply also to an organizational system.

The Syndrome applies where a person, usually the senior in status, age or both, is in a position of responsibility or control over another person. A sense of exploitation exists if failure to comply with a

---

3   Summit, R.C. (1983) 'The Child Sexual Abuse Accommodation Syndrome' *Child Abuse and Neglect*, 7, 177–193.

request or a directive implies a further, secondary, threat for the 'junior' person. Again this might be, for example, loss of job, finance, or other loss of care and support.

Example: A situation we encountered at one point, with details suitably changed, illustrates the helplessness of someone in a subordinate position. The caretaker of a care home lived in a flat attached to the home. When he was asked in future to take his time off in three half days each week, he talked to the chair of the committee who oversaw his work. Not having a full day off would prevent him playing snooker matches, or visiting his elderly mother, his only close relative who lived some distance away. He was told that if he was unhappy with his conditions he was free to resign.

He knew that similar posts were limited in that area and felt he must accommodate to the 'injunction' rather than lose his job and his home. After several weeks of anxiety, waiting to see if the decision might be reversed, he spoke to his union representative who discussed the situation with the committee on his behalf. His own appeal had been rejected but advocacy by someone with a different authority enabled the situation to be resolved.

Summit points out that a person is psychologically orphaned if they have felt in some way exploited and their plea for support to someone else in authority is rejected. An alternative to disclosure of the problem therefore may be to submit to the situation because of fear of blame or punishment. Even if a statement or complaint is made, it may be retracted because the person feels unable to cope with accusations of manipulation, exaggeration, attempting to cause division, or even lying.

People in a subordinate position face a secondary trauma at the point of disclosure if they are faced with an inconsistent intervention system. If no one in authority intervenes to acknowledge the reality of the experience, the person is put on the defensive. They may be seen as attacking the credibility of someone who has control or authority, and possibly creating a crisis of loyalty within the organization. There is then a tendency on the part of the person experiencing the difficulty 'to deal with the trauma with ... guilt, self-blame, panic and rage'.

If, on the other hand, someone in an appropriate position of authority can advocate for them and protect against the exploitation or unrealistic expectation, this seems to confer on the person 'the power to be self-endorsing and to recover with minimum consequences'.

Summit suggested that the Accommodation Syndrome included five categories, reflecting compelling reality for those experiencing lack of advocacy.

- Secrecy;
- Helplessness;
- Entrapment and accommodation;
- Delayed, conflicted and unconvincing disclosure;
- Retraction.

1. Clergy families, advocacy and 'nowhere to be heard'

The interviews showed that often the families felt they had to accommodate to demands or difficult situations when efforts to resolve them failed.

Example: A family with three children under six arrived in the husband's first parish as incumbent to find a filthy house with urgent repairs and preparations, including a new kitchen, hardly started.

A senior member of their congregation was on the Parsonages Board so they spoke to him about the severe difficulties the situation was causing for the family and the priest's job. They did not know how persistent to be in a new diocese and thought that he might be able to intervene on their behalf. They waited. Apparently he took no action but, in particular, he gave them no feedback and the situation remained unchanged. If they approached the bishop, they could be seen to be complaining.

A second concurrent issue was that the four churches in the parish had completely split over traditional or charismatic forms of worship, emphasizing other differences. In his first incumbency he was immediately being asked to resolve major conflict. Over a year later, the Rural Dean asked how he was managing to deal with the complexities he faced and how he had survived. He seemed well informed about what had been happening, but had offered no support or consultation. He also implied that others in the diocese knew of the situation, but no one had discussed it with him.

The Accommodation Syndrome has been applicable in a variety of situations for other professions in our experience of workplace counselling over many years. With the difficulties of this example in mind, we examined Summit's five categories for clergy families.

2. The way the Accommodation Syndrome applies

● *Secrecy*

Summit points out that people in subordinate positions are mainly dependent on their seniors' explanation for the reality assigned to an experience 'however logical or illogical that may be'. This may be stated or implied. If the family described above, for instance, fail to cope without complaining, the implication may be that previous clergy have coped. They may be seen as unwilling to accept sacrifice, or even as having too little faith. They may then feel it is better to say nothing more, especially in a new parish and diocese.

'The secrecy is, therefore, both the source of fear and the promise of safety – "everything will be all right if you just don't tell". Any attempt to throw light on the exploitation may be met with silence and disbelief.'

● *Helplessness*

The belief held by many people that people generally have an inbuilt sense of self-protection and would naturally disclose exploitation 'ignores the basic subordination and helplessness within authoritarian relationships'. It is important, therefore, for the degree of someone's dependency to be acknowledged in assessing any situation. For clergy families, after ordination, most aspects of their lives are dependent on the church at different levels as the data show.

Summit goes on to say that many people 'tend to despise helplessness and condemn anyone who submits too easily to intimidation' without necessarily stopping to assess the overall complexity of the situation.

● *Entrapment and accommodation*

If an appropriate person to whom exploitation or unrealistic expectations are disclosed does not provide protective intervention or act as advocate for the 'junior' person then 'the only healthy option is to learn to accept the situation and survive'. This leads to a classic role reversal. Responsibility for 'good results' to emerge from the situation is left with the dependent person rather than with those who should bear the responsibility.

Summit suggests that in the process of accommodating to the situation, where necessary protection is ignored, people will develop mechanisms to cope, but these survival skills become handicaps to effective ongoing psychological health. Accommodation mechanisms can be overcome only if the person 'can be led to trust in a secure environment, which can provide consistent, non-contingent acceptance and caring'. Naturally, the 'non-contingent' aspect would have limitations in an organizational or work context, but providing a secure base will be discussed in Chapter 12.

When these mechanisms fail, the 'intolerance of helplessness and the increasing feeling of rage will seek active expression. The rage may incubate over years of façade and coping' and may erupt as a pattern of exploitation in turn against those in the future who are dependent on them. Avenues of escape may include drink or drugs.

- *Delayed, conflicted and unconvincing disclosure*
Exploitation may never be disclosed. On the other hand disclosure may be triggered only after conflict in the situation finally leads to a breakdown of accommodation mechanisms. If this happens, the person will be seeking understanding and intervention in an atmosphere of tension at the very time when they are least likely to find them.

An alternative accommodation pattern exists in which the person succeeds in hiding any indication of conflict by being unusually achieving and popular, eager to please both those in authority and their peers. Any disclosure of ongoing exploitation then produces even greater incredulity, as 'obviously' the situation has done no harm.

- *Retraction*
Even if a person discloses the exploitation, they may reverse their statement. There can be a sense of confusion, guilt or self-doubt about the way the situation has arisen and the intention of the 'senior' person. Particularly for clergy and their families, they may bear the responsibility of keeping 'the family' together, again not only their own but the wider Christian or congregational family. As Summit says, 'the role reversal continues with the 'bad' choice being to tell the truth and the 'good' choice being to capitulate and restore a lie for the sake of the family'.

III. REFLECTIONS

The Accommodation Syndrome as outlined by Summit relates
particularly to situations where the 'junior' person anticipates a
trusting relationship with the person in authority. A particular issue
for clergy families is that they expect such a trusting relationship with
those in authority around them. The family assume that there will be
at least some concern for their welfare, for instance, in the parish
situation outlined above for the family with young children. The lack
of both action and communication in both the personal and the
professional situations they faced reflects disbelief from others that the
situation is as difficult as outlined by the family.

Part of the difficulty may be that the Leadership Group tended to
see this need for advocacy and support only within the framework of
dependency. The Group stated very emphatically that they wished
that clergy and their families would be more independent. They also
said (and this was echoed by bishops we met in the USA) that it was
not possible for bishops to take on the dual role of pastoral carer and
disciplinarian.

The Canons of the Church of England[4] speak of a bishop as 'The
chief pastor of all that are within his diocese ... and their father in
God' and bishops often refer to themselves in this way. At the
induction service for an incumbent of a parish the bishop says, 'Take
the cure of souls which is *your care and mine*'. Clergy therefore have a
sense of working in partnership with the bishop. The example above
suggests that this does not necessarily happen in practice even in such
demanding situations.

The families too saw the bishop as their 'Father in God', and
anticipated a pastoral role from him. Given the schedules the bishops
described, it would be unrealistic for them to fulfil a pastoral role in a
direct sense, but any structures for communication and practical help
that might provide that role were mostly obscure or not easily
available. There was little or no evidence of the families looking for
over-protection, but rather a need for the dependence of the families
in many situations to be acknowledged. The interviews showed
various instances of the families feeling 'psychologically orphaned'
when they raised concerns and were ignored. The lack of appropriate

4 *Canons of the Church of England.* (1975) London, CIO Publishing.

advocacy or even guidance was striking in many instances so there was no one 'to confer on the person the power to be self-endorsing and to recover with minimum consequences'.

So clergy and the families were receiving another implicit, if not explicit, contrary message, 'be independent' on the one hand, and 'the task is shared' on the other. This is another instance of the Double Bind. The hypothesis that clergy families are caught in that Bind and may find their only possible response is in terms of the Accommodation Syndrome would be explored further in the second and third interviews.

12 Yardsticks for Independence

Other ideas that we explored at this stage, especially those about independence and expectations, are themes underlying discussions by the families and the two Groups throughout the interviews. These were viewed in a range of different ways and seemed to spring mainly from the personal agenda of individual parish members or groups. The ideas may or may not be relevant to the person or situation to which they are applied but this does not diminish their strength.

We looked at a number of theories to provide yardsticks for both independence and expectations.

I. INDEPENDENCE

1. Independence or inappropriate demand?

As we have seen, each part of the research viewed independence from a different perspective. At their first meeting, the Leadership Group emphasized that they were keen for clergy not to 'perpetuate inappropriate dependency' and looked for them to exercise much greater independence.

The interviews showed the complications for both clergy and family members of trying to act independently. They felt that at each of the early stages of ministry – selection for ordination, training, and appointment to a curacy – the structures were unclear and varied significantly from diocese to diocese. Lack of communication at all levels added to the difficulty of knowing how to proceed across a range of issues.

Independence given to the *laity*, for example, responsibility for curates' housing and paying expenses, may undermine the independence that clergy attempt to exercise and put clergy in the dual roles of leadership and dependency simultaneously. This situation was mentioned by the Pastoral Group but does not appear to be recognized or acknowledged generally.

Despite formal and informal promises, situations were often only addressed when the families themselves attempted to find an appropriate solution, that is, to act independently. The diocese, parish or senior staff might not consider that the family's solutions *were* appropriate. A senior bishop's comments at a commissioning service for Church Army officers, reported in the *Church Times*,[1] illustrates the dilemma.

'He said that too many priests were making "quite extraordinary demands" about where they should live. "We are in danger of losing the sacrificial elements of our calling and our sending"'.

'His remarks had been provoked by a run of people over three or four years who "get me a bit on edge", such as curates who say, "I need a house of such-and-such proportions, with so many rooms, in such a location", rather than, "I'm ready to respond to what the Church itself wants, or you as bishop feels is right". Obviously there was a balance to be drawn but he was getting a sense that clergy were "no longer putting themselves at the disposal of the Church" as in previous generations'.

The first letter in response to the Report a week later was from a clergy wife.

'Giving up control of your life and "putting (yourself) at the disposal of the Church" is a risky and uncomfortable business that may yield great rewards and/or unbearable stresses ... To be on the receiving end, at one remove, of the appointments procedure is to feel like an insignificant and easily overlooked part of the jigsaw.

'Some clergy households, like ours, will need to set their own boundaries in terms of location, housing and schooling. This should be welcomed as active participation in the process, not seen as a negative approach. I need to safeguard my interests and the

---

1 *Church Times,* ' Report of Ordination Service in Sheffield Cathedral', 28 June 1996.

interests of our children. The Church cannot take account of these unless there is some way of making them known.'

A parish clergyman wrote:

'I am not opposed to the language of sacrifice. Too often, however, it is used as a cover for the effects of mismanagement and pastoral insensitivity. Stipendiary ministers give up a great deal in terms of income and free time. But are they called to sacrifice marriages and health as well?'

An Archdeacon's letter said:

'The Bishop may be right, but only to a degree. I have been amazed and very humbled by the number of clergy, men and women, single or with a family, who courageously face the prospect of vandalism, burglary and personal injury in our urban areas. Their demands are only for the protection of their families and their churches.'

The correspondence highlights a finding of the American Episcopal Families Network[2] research, discussed in Chapter 5, that there is 'no theology of the married priesthood. There needs to be a sound theological basis for the integration of the dual sacraments of marriage and ordination, to put to rest the ambivalence and struggle with which so many have lived for so long'.

2.   Independence and the freehold

The Pastoral Group were concerned that the historic independence of the freehold, discussed in Chapter 2, which gave clergy the legal right to remain in their parishes, could leave clergy isolated. Individual clergy might have different priorities to those in neighbouring parishes, but comparisons might still be made between the size of congregation, the level of giving, involvement in the community or other issues. No account might be taken of the broader context, as even neighbouring parishes could be very diverse.

---

2   Episcopal Families Network (1988) *Episcopal Clergy Families in the '80s*. New York: The Episcopal Church Foundation.

The Group saw the cycle of stress that could result. They felt such comparisons were damaging. They could lead to a sense of rivalry or failure unless clergy had supervision or consultation to put the situation in perspective. The resulting frustration or anger could lead to all the risks of inappropriate behaviour, depression or the breakdown of ministry. Their isolation then acted as a means of keeping these carefully hidden. The Pastoral Group also thought that clergy only seek their help when these situations become critical. Their comments linked closely with the secrecy of the Double Bind and the Accommodation Syndrome and suggested that independence can be a two-edged sword.

Even with the withdrawal of the freehold, and the setting up of Team and Group ministries, the families' comments suggested that they could still be left feeling isolated, without support or encouragement.

3. Independence and the overall picture

The families spoke of times when they received much care and thought from individual parishioners and from church officials. The greatest difficulty was that no one took their whole situation into account, not only for clergy families generally but also for each specific family. This was especially true if families changed dioceses. When this happened, those who had known of situations that a family had faced in the past, such as parish complications or personal tragedy, would no longer have an influence on that family's position.

The concept of independence can be more complex than is often acknowledged. What emerges, in terms of human resource management, is the key importance of good two-way communication and co-ordination. Clergy and laity each need to fulfil their part in a balance of responsibility, with the leadership at each level considering the whole situation for each individual clergy family when issues arise.

II.   A SECURE BASE AND EMPOWERMENT

1.   The theory of a secure base

As part of the context in which people are expected to be

independent, we explored Bowlby's[3] ideas of a secure base. We realized that if these were applied to the whole system of the Church, they could help to shed light on clergy families' situation.

Bowlby developed his well-known theories of attachment and a secure base in the field of child development and parenting. The ideas emerged, however, from two sources. One was his wartime experience; the other was working with a group of psychiatrists[4] who had brought a new approach to human resource problems facing the army after World War II. Using their professional skills of listening and establishing trust, they went into the field to discover the most pressing problems of commanding officers, and to 'identify a path of solution'. They then developed a model of the necessary remedial measures and trained army personnel to occupy the required roles. These psychiatrists also developed similar projects in post-war years in a variety of industrial settings.

Bowlby used the analogy of a military base. This has a key role in maintaining a good communications link with those on the front line, otherwise the base will not provide security. Mostly the base will have a static but vital waiting role. 'Only when that officer is confident his base is secure dare he press forward and take risks.'[5]

2. Application of the secure base theory

Several points discussed by Bowlby would apply to stress for clergy families and the response of the wider church.

● *Communication*

The psychiatrists working with the Army used their 'professional skills of listening and establishing trust'. They worked in collaboration with commanding officers so that 'constructive ideas about dealing with human resource problems would emerge'. This suggests that

3 Bowlby, J. (1988) *A Secure Base: Clinical Applications of Attachment Theory*. London: Routledge.
4 Trist, E. and Murray, H. (1990) 'Historical Overview: The Foundation and Development of the Tavistock Institute to 1989', in E. Trist and H. Murray (eds) *The Social Engagement of Social Science Vol I: The Socio-Psychological Perspective*. London: Free Association Books.
5 The concept of a secure base was developed by General Wingate in WWII. Such bases were established behind Japanese lines in the Far East to attack enemy lines of communication.

these constructive ideas were hammered out together through prolonged contact and discussion. The officers were not simply left to work out the ideas for themselves.

● *Encouragement*
Bowlby says that, 'in essence this role of providing a secure base is one of being available, ready to respond when called upon to encourage and perhaps assist but to intervene actively only when clearly necessary'. This implies that if a response of encouragement is readily available and natural in the situation, the need to intervene is likely to be less frequent. He does not suggest that this would preclude discipline or instruction if these were appropriate, but does suggest that encouragement is likely to lead to greater clarity and independence.

● *Independence*
Bowlby indicates that a secure base is in fact the *starting point* for independence and from this will spring the courage to 'press forward and take risks'.

● *Empowerment*
The themes of two books tie these ideas together. First, Herriott and Pemberton consider good communication to be the starting point for feeling empowered at work.[6] They suggest that employees should be more proactive when discussing job opportunities and training with managers. This would give them insight into the objectives of the organization as a basis for new initiatives and independent decisions.

Secondly, West and Farr suggest that security is the primary condition necessary for innovation and creativity at work.[7] They consider employees are very vulnerable if difficulties arise from their independent initiatives without a degree of security and a sense of management support.

The third interviews show that a particular concern for the clergy in their next five years would be the lack of 'support and

---

6 Herriott, P. and Pemberton, C. (1995) *New Deals: the Revolution in Managerial Careers*. Chichester: Wiley.
7 West, M. A. and Farr, J. L. (1990) *Innovation and Creativity at Work*. Chichester: Wiley.

reinforcement that you would have in a secular job'. They were very unsure if leaders knew them well enough to discuss their future ministry in a constructive way. If clergy have little opportunity for regular discussion with the leadership, how would they know what would be considered appropriate in terms of innovation and independence? There was little sense of a secure base.

III. THE DOUGHNUT PRINCIPLE

Even so, clergy were pressing forward and attempting to fulfil their task satisfactorily. Charles Handy, who wrote the classic text, *Understanding Organisations*,[8] has always had a concern for the context in which people work. In *The Empty Raincoat*[9] he links empowerment to the 'Doughnut Principle'.

The idea is of an inside-out doughnut with the hole on the outside as a bounded space and the dough or core in the middle. The core 'contains all the things which have to be done in a job or role if you are not to fail ... your duties. The core, however, is not the whole doughnut. There is, thankfully, the space beyond. This space is our opportunity to make a difference ... to live up to our full potential'.

Handy suggests that the doughnut can represent a relationship or an organization or work group 'just as we can use it to reveal the balance in our own life between work and family or between necessity and choice'.

However, he goes on to suggest that there are some whose jobs are nearly all space with little core and no boundary. He gives just one example. 'Ministers of religion have a visible core to their work – the church services, some sick visits, committees and finances – but there is no limit to their responsibilities for the souls of the congregation or for their evangelizing work. Some of the most stressed people that I have known have been people with jobs like these, because there is no end, no way in which you can look back and say, "It was a great year", because it could always have been greater. Empowerment, in a sense, has gone too far. Without a boundary it is easy to be oppressed by

8 Handy, C. (1976, 1985) *Understanding Organisations*. London: Penguin.
9 Handy, C. (1994) *The Empty Raincoat: Making Sense of the Future*. London: Hutchinson.

guilt, for enough is never enough… A sensible job is a balanced doughnut'. It is interesting that for him, as a clergy son, the ministry is the prime example of an unbalanced job, which echoes all that our families said.

Again, the message is that independence and empowerment need defined boundaries, and these contribute significantly to the provision of a secure base for clergy as for all employees. Otherwise, as Handy points out, clergy are left with 'the constant wearing down process' from the general pressure of such a diffuse job, without encouragement and without feedback to know if it is aptly focused or 'a failure'.

IV. EXPECTATIONS – PEOPLE BEFORE THE PUBLIC

The first interviews showed that family members could be expected to be available on demand, to do certain things or behave in particular ways, as though they needed to meet some unspecified ideal. Logan Pearsall Smith[10] points out the significant effect this type of idealistic expectation has on those in the public eye. 'People before the public live an imagined life in the thoughts of others and flourish or feel faint as they grow bright or dwindle in that mirror'.

In other words, people have a particular image of how public figures should live their lives. The self-image of those figures then rises and falls, reflecting the approval or disapproval they experience from those around them. The difficulty is that there is not just one mirror that reflects public expectations generally, but an endless hall of mirrors, as many as the numbers of the public.

The Pastoral Group's suggestion that clergy families need to learn to 'deal with' the many different expectations they face may then be more complicated than it appears. Family members can develop general strategies but each expectation has a particular focus and setting so has to be dealt with separately. As we have seen the families were also very conscious of being on the front line in representing the Christian faith to the public. This makes the expectations more difficult to shrug off.

---

10 Pearsall Smith, L. (1933) 'Afterthoughts from *All Trivia*'. London: Constable & Company Ltd. Quoted in Preface to R. Hoggart, (1992) *An Imagined Life*. London: Chatto & Windus.

A letter to the *Daily Telegraph* from Lord Habgood in April 1997, shows how the personal and therefore the family lives of clergy are still expected by the public to be included in their role. 'Clergy fall into a different category, not because there are different standards of morality for clergy and laity, but because they are public figures whose actions and lifestyle are rightly seen as representing the mind of the Church. In a matter which is doubtful, they have a responsibility not to pre-empt any final decision, and should not exercise the freedom of conscience enjoyed by others. This may seem hard, but it is no different from the constraints placed on many other public figures in moral matters which might have repercussions on their professional role.'

In the midst of the expectations, the family are still a family dealing with their own relationships and needs. When Walsh[11] reviewed ideas of family life, she concluded that 'there are many pathways to healthy family functioning' which can take very diverse forms. This flexibility for each family to find their own path at every stage is lost if an ever-changing ideal is imposed. The children's frustration in particular showed how damaging this could be.

V. REFLECTIONS

When all that the families said is put alongside the ideas discussed in these two chapters, and issues of stress in Chapter 3, a pattern begins to emerge.

At an early stage the families became aware that a wide variety of people saw them as role models and tried to impose an ideal image on them. As public figures they faced many expectations and contrary messages. The Pastoral Group said they needed to learn to deal with these, but the data suggested that the whole issue of expectations was like quicksand. An opportunity to discuss this, and other issues linked to being in the public eye, could help them to articulate particular complications that these expectations caused. Such discussion would also address the secrecy of the Double Bind and the Accommodation Syndrome.

---

11 Walsh, F. (1993) 'Conceptualisation of normal family processes', in F. Walsh (ed.) *Normal Family Processes* (2nd edn). London: Guilford Press.

We have seen how the families tried to fulfil the expectation not to maintain 'inappropriate dependency'. However, Bowlby demonstrates that the *starting point* for independence is a secure base, with good communication and encouragement as essential strands. For the families these ingredients are almost entirely absent. Curates had little opportunity for individual discussion with the leadership to have 'greater clarity' about the task. Training vicars had very individual ideas about how their task should be fulfilled, so they might not talk to curates about a wide variety of issues in the important early stages of ministry.

It is interesting that none of the elements of independence discussed in this chapter suggest an individual autonomy, although independence is so often viewed in this way. They suggest instead a whole process of two-way communication within the organization to help 'employees' to understand its goals and structures, and the boundaries and flexibility these imply at each level. The clear guidelines outlined by this process would then provide the secure base from which clergy, as with any employees, would be able to act independently.

Otherwise, the Doughnut Principle comes into play and, as Handy points out, clergy then remain 'among the most stressed professionals'. They are left with 'the constant wearing down process' from the general pressure of such a diffuse job, without encouragement and without feedback to know if it is aptly focused or 'a failure'. Their family in turn are left as their main 'professional' support 'to find a path to solution' but with little control over most situations. They spoke of the stress that this produced.

The ideas from both these chapters will form a background as we continue to think about the links between independence and a secure base, and the importance of a balanced job. The effect of management expecting independence, without appropriate support and boundaries, will also be explored further in the next rounds of interviews, as well as the impact on the families of living in the public eye with all the expectations involved.

PART FIVE
The Incumbency Stage

13 Moves and Education

I. THE SECOND INTERVIEWS

A striking finding from the first interviews was that the dedication of clergy and their families to the priest's vocation was undiminished in spite of a dearth of encouragement, and limited management and support structures. Their determination and sense of purpose remained intact but their main resources continued to be their own mental and spiritual capacity and the support of their families. They were aware that over time these could be gradually undermined by the weight of their responsibilities.

At the end of Chapter 12 we saw how the different theories we had explored formed a coherent framework. The lack of a secure base caused considerable stress for all the family and made it difficult for clergy to act independently. There was no available forum for regular discussion of the issues they encountered in all the diversity of the job. This uncertain silence left clergy attempting to fulfil their ordination vows largely alone with very few guidelines.

The Reference Groups had been concerned at the degree of stress and isolation that the families experienced. In the light of the complications the families faced, one of our supervisors had asked, 'What are the pay-offs?' The Leadership Group had said it would be helpful to look at how clergy families function generally. Putting these comments together we focused the second interviews on the positives of clergy family life to help us find a rounded view of the families' experience.

Our open-ended questions were relevant to children of all ages and led to wide-ranging conversations with the families. We asked:

What do you like about your family?
What would you prefer not to have to do?

In both cases they were asked:

Is that because you are a clergy family or is there some other reason?

Interviews again took place in the families' homes, wherever they now were in the country, with the whole family together. We began by reviewing events for the family over the year since the previous interview.

This showed how the families had dealt with many serious issues during that time. Frequently, work issues came to the priest at the house, so all members could become involved. For instance, one clergy wife spoke of the suicide of a parishioner shortly before we met, 'which came right into our home'. She was in the house on her own with three small children when a church member brought the news, and they had to talk within the children's hearing.

Incidents like this illustrated the way the family never knew when they might be caught up in such events. Visitors in emotional turmoil may pour out their concerns to the first member of the family they see, and may not be aware or take account of children overhearing their conversations and the impact this may have.

II.   THE PAY-OFFS

The interviews ranged over all aspects of family life. They showed a deep commitment to one another within the family. They liked the general support they gave each other and the way they encouraged one another to be themselves. For instance, three of the older teenagers from different families went to other churches where they could have their own identity and be more independent.

The families laughed and teased, debated and disagreed during the interviews in an open and natural way, indicating that children were encouraged to have their own opinions. The data also showed that at times tempers flared and rows ensued, especially with the teenagers. The Pastoral Group commented on the positive effect of clergy children learning to mix with people of all ages from an early stage, and this may have helped them to express themselves so clearly.

One younger teenager said she liked the way her older brother would acknowledge her in school in front of his friends and talk to her. 'Most other brothers don't'. They enjoyed the encouragement they received in all their interests. Six of the children played sport at county level or had won national awards; others had done well in drama, ballet and music.

The parents valued the privilege of sharing so many people's lives at key moments through weddings, baptisms and funerals. They valued, too, the very natural opportunities their position gave them to talk to other people about faith, and the privilege of being 'set aside' and so having time to do this. The whole family appreciated the warmth and friendship they received from the church family.

The catch-up session at the beginning of each round suggested they were keenly aware of each other's achievements and disappointments. The parents were surprised how much even small children remembered about them and touched by perceptive comments from children of all ages: 'I didn't know you knew me that well!'

They were very adaptable to the ever-changing patterns within the family, often dictated by the clergy job, and very involved in one another's lives. There were many indications that they knew each other's strengths and limitations, likes and dislikes and were aware of their moods, hopes and fears, as well as their vulnerabilities. Mostly there were clear and appropriate boundaries between parents and children. All these positive aspects of their family life were emphasized at this point in answer to our question, but were also mentioned at each stage of the interviews.

They felt that almost all the things they liked about their family were because they were a family together with a lot of care and concern for one another. In most instances they thought it was not just being a clergy family but that it would be the same if they were a Christian family doing secular jobs.

The difference came when we asked what they would prefer not to have to do. Washing-up, of course, and keeping their rooms *and* the whole house tidy which was emphasized because they never knew when people would be coming. This was just one aspect among many others of being on show as a public family and exposed to so many expectations and criticisms. In particular, they disliked having to carry things back and forth to church week after week and take part in church events for other age groups. They hated having to keep quiet if there were meetings in the house and people thinking of them differently because they were a clergy family.

As they talked, we bore in mind the main building blocks for families to function in a healthy way: good communication, and mostly the stability, yet flexibility, so important to individual development. All this could be undermined or disrupted at any time by the constant pressures and demands of the job. The following chapters will show how the cumulative effect of stress of the Double ABCX Model, outlined in Chapter 5, affected their family life. This accumulation is often hidden from those around them and not discussed beyond the family, so this was the first opportunity many of them had to share their experiences.

Their discussions echoed issues they raised in earlier chapters, but at this stage of their ministry they had a significant, longer-term influence.

III. MOVES

The families spoke more to us about moves than anything else. Once a priest became an incumbent, responsibility for the parish would be on the doorstep as soon as he arrived. If the moves were difficult, every aspect of the family's life would be affected. All the families said that again at this stage they had little control over most aspects of their moves, however carefully they planned. As we have seen, lack of control was a key element of stress, and made independent action to overcome stress far more difficult. This would account for the fact that moves were such a major concern for all the families.

In today's society few professional employees who accept a job have to move to a specific house in a specific place irrespective of its suitability for the family. This may mean, for clergy, that a suitable job is not taken because the house is inappropriate for that family at that time.

On the other hand, clergy may feel they should accept a parish for a wide variety of other reasons such as school stages for children and the care of elderly parents. It is this all-encompassing situation – the job and the specific house, as well as all the family considerations – that makes moves for clergy families so complex. However, the prime consideration, as the interviews showed, would still be the job itself. All other aspects of the situation would have to fit in.

1.   Independence and fragmentation

There was no one responsible for co-ordinating the process of moving to ensure that work on the house was carried out or that the family was kept in touch with progress. The clergy families' dilemma was how far they could put pressure, however reasonable, on diocesan or parish officials without creating the wrong impression about their whole ministry. This was especially so if they moved to a different diocese and did not know the staff or normal channels for communication. Ad hoc decisions might be made at diocesan or parish level with only one or two aspects of the family's situation in focus.

2.   The moves themselves

A Trust appointed one vicar, but the stipulation was that a new incumbent must be instituted within a year of the parish becoming vacant or the bishop could appoint his own candidate. The bishop had an alternative priest in mind so this vicar had to be instituted in time. His daughter had an emergency admission to hospital just before the due date and was critically ill, but the institution had to go ahead or he would have lost the job. He left his very sick child and her anxious mother behind.

One of the most difficult experiences has been outlined in Chapter 7 as an example of the Accommodation Syndrome. Here it is given in more detail to show some of the practical dilemmas families face during moves if agreed work on a vicarage is not carried out. The couple described the move to their first parish as 'catastrophic'. 'The kitchen was 'a dead loss and the Parsonages Board agreed six months before we went that something should be done.' Dates for the work were agreed and confirmed but the work didn't start till a week before they moved and it continued for several weeks after. They explained their situation to a member of the Parsonages Board who was in their new congregation and asked for his help but nothing was done and nothing was said. They had three children under six, including a baby.

In line with national practice on moving (The Green Guide), they had asked for certain much needed re-decorating to be done. This was the responsibility of the parish. Work had been done for the previous incumbent but, as he had not stayed 'long', the parish decided it shouldn't be done again, even though a parishioner had volunteered to decorate some rooms and marked the agreed colours on the walls in indelible felt-tipped pen. 'In the end only the upstairs ceilings were done, very badly.' The felt-tipped notes remained.

The husband had not known until the research interview two or three years later that his wife had been asked not to say anything by the Rural Dean who might have talked to the parish. She said that the Rural Dean was in a very awkward position because he had had to deal with the situation during the interregnum. The 'awkward position' for the family was therefore lost to view.

'Nobody from the congregation came near the vicarage.' Later, parishioners said they thought the family wanted to be left alone to settle in. 'The house was dirty, the garden a jungle and the garage had two years of newspapers in it'. They found a total divide between the four parishes. Although this was his first living, the husband had no diocesan support or advice in dealing with the conflict.

It was interesting that the husband had hesitated to take part in the research because he felt his contemporaries from college sometimes moaned too much. After they had described their experience his wife said, 'We've put it behind us now'. She paused, and added, '. . . but because there was nowhere to talk about it, it is still there'.

Personally and professionally we have frequently been told of still more complicated moves, which took longer to resolve. In these instances families have lived in chaos for weeks, if not months. The Leadership Group in their session said that archdeacons have an important role over clergy homes. The Diocesan Secretary is the chief executive on diocesan housing. Decisions on housing are made by the Parsonages Committee with input by the surveyors and archdeacons.

In all the conversations about moves and housing, the families did not appear to know how the Parsonages Committee operated. They did not seem to be aware that it would be more appropriate to take housing issues, when there were problems, to the Diocesan Secretary rather than the bishop.

3. The possibility of moves

There was always the possibility of unexpected moves as the couples wanted to be sensitive to God's call and guidance. A potential job change was unsettling to the families, even if the post were not offered or accepted.

At times, personal advice from mentors meant clergy spent time considering unlikely jobs. After five years in his parish, one priest was asked to look at a job in the couple's original home area. His former vicar and his college tutor, now a bishop, encouraged him to 'go for it'. His wife felt the timing was quite wrong, couldn't believe he would consider it and they didn't speak for two days.

By the time she had decided it was right to consider the post, her husband emerged from a PCC meeting saying they had voted to go ahead with a long-planned parish pilgrimage which he had initiated and he couldn't possibly leave. Despite his sense of certainty, he became unsettled.

They felt encouraged that their current bishop asked him to consider a parish with a larger staff a year later. They did not accept it but the move they chose for family considerations of health and schooling proved difficult and unfulfilling. For all the families there was always this risk of 'getting it wrong'. Three years later this family moved again.

Unknown to applicants, there may also be personal agendas behind the scenes of any job advertisement, such as the bishop's candidate who was asked to consider the parish in the paragraph above.

4.   Ambivalence and personal agendas

Teenage children expressed both anger and helplessness when moves disrupted their lives, but these affected parents too. One father told us, 'Several times I just sat down and cried as my son was distraught at moving. I felt, "how could I do this to him?" It wasn't like the bank moving you because you'd got promotion. I found it very difficult that it was my choice because I couldn't cope with the parish situation any longer. And I was putting my children, especially him, through this traumatic time.' Another father whose children had found their current parish very difficult said there must be a pay-off for the children in their next move.

One incumbent felt very let down by a minimal attendance at a special meeting with diocesan representatives present, and thought he might move sooner than planned. His wife was more cautious, seeing the attractions and dangers of moving when things are discouraging. She was not at that moment physically capable of handling a move because of back problems, but he was concentrating more on the decision-making process.

Several incumbents confirmed one man's suggestion that 'the going rate is about ten years' for staying in a parish. A wife commented, 'Because of the energy needed to stay on top in this parish, we would expect to be moving in five years'. Another incumbent hoped to move to a non-parish appointment after a long spell in urban parishes. One wife saw a move as a way of clearing the decks of commitments.

As clergy made plans about how long to stay, children joked about dreams of 'the bishop's fabulous job offer' but one man who was at odds with his bishop had a different perspective. 'If I upset him too much I don't suppose we'll move at all.' Any job application would require his bishop's reference.

5. Specific advice or an overall picture? providing a secure base

Several discussions during the interviews suggested that leaders had given advice based on their own experience without acknowledging the current overall circumstances for that family. One man was offered a parish in another diocese where there had been a long interregnum so the bishop there wanted him to move quickly. 'We had a parish mission coming up and a baby about to be born so I didn't want to move until the summer. After talking to two bishops and an archdeacon we moved before both.'

His wife said, 'That was very, very hard. A lot of stress came out of that later because of being in a new parish with a new baby without friendships and networks set up. We suddenly had a new role in a vicarage not a curate's house and this was our first child. I ended up getting post-natal depression, which we acknowledged about a year later. I'm sure all those things contributed.'

From the husband's point of view the personal touch of a letter from the bishop saying he himself had moved just before having a baby persuaded him to toe the line. He did not say whether the bishop and his wife had also been moving to an inner city area, to their first parish with their first baby. Members of their previous parish said, 'We wish you'd stayed. She's our baby really' (an interesting perspective on being a public family). 'And bereavement from us', the husband said, 'because we'd formed a lot of close relationships there'.

Had anyone understood their pressures and isolation, and offered support? Their new suffragan bishop had. He had visited them after the baby was born and they had talked to him and his wife a year later.

'This was when I was acknowledging that I was depressed. I also saw a psychiatrist in outpatients but actually the whole business of acknowledging anything ...' Who else had been aware of their situation? 'No-one', she said, 'we don't see them frequently enough. It was for us to say help, not for them to say you may need extra support'. The husband had known the suffragan bishop and had talked to him over several years. He said, 'I suppose I had a sense of trust that if and when we really needed to, there was someone we could go to'.

There were a number of times throughout the interviews, during tense or difficult conversations like this one, when family members left sentences unfinished. 'Acknowledging anything ...'

Their story raises a number of issues. Are there times when leaders, after speaking to priests about their situation, might suggest that the family needs protecting from unrealistic demands, so a job offer should not be taken further or the institution delayed?

In *Living with Stress,* Dr Sarah Horsman[1] suggests that 'handled badly, the many potential areas of loss entailed in moving can be a threat to physical and mental health'. She goes on to say, 'If you are a minister faced with such a situation, it is important to *seek* help (her italics) from friends, family, or caring agencies'. The data suggest that this links with the accepted culture of independence in the Church. If clergy and families are expected to *seek* help, does this mean that help may not be offered even in the circumstances this couple faced – 'It was for us to say help, not for them to say you need support.' If so, should this be an area that the leadership re-examine?

The potential for help for this couple 'without friendships and networks set up' was obviously limited. The move had come quickly with little space to adjust, so they had all the potential of threat to mental health outlined above. Their wider families lived at a considerable distance and were sceptical of the church, which had led to uneasy relationships. Contact with personal friends was limited.

If no one in an official position has acknowledged their situation and actually offered support, it may be very difficult for clergy families to *ask* for help. It could reflect on the priest's work and commitment, if they admit they are struggling, making it doubly difficult. The

---

1   Horsman, S. (1989) *Living with Stress, A Guide for Ministers and Church Leaders.* Cambridge: Lutterworth Press.

Leadership's subsequent discussion on failure and weakness in this round of interviews would seem to confirm this.

Even after she needed psychiatric help, who would decide that this was the point to talk to the suffragan bishop? Would that be up to the wife, conscious of the possible effect on her husband's job? This couple would also be going to a bishop known to the husband for a number of years. Without this personal contact and 'sense of trust' it may have been even harder for the wife to admit her need. The interviews and this priests' subsequent appointment suggested that the hierarchy saw them as an able couple.

Two particular factors may influence the Church's attitude to providing support. One is the pressure of the job for bishops and other leaders. It is unrealistic to think that the suffragan bishop could have monitored the situation for this couple adequately himself. What other mechanisms were in place to provide such monitoring? The question remains whether *this* couple should have been asked to go to *this* parish at *that* particular moment. How far should an organization take responsibility for its demands, especially when the family are in the public domain?

6. The need for co-ordination and planning

There were two other types of situation where organizational pressure was transferred to the families. The first was pressure to move quickly for three families, because delay and lack of forethought elsewhere in the system had allowed a successor to be appointed before housing was ready for the outgoing family. In two cases, the priest travelled daily from an original job to the new job. This included meetings till 10 in the evening. In one instance it was for a month, in the other for six months as no suitable house could be found. This family was left in a 'kind of limbo' after leaving, but not physically leaving, the previous parish. There was no record of the stress caused to those waiting in the wings for the houses to be vacated.

In the second situation a suffragan bishop lost sight of the general needs of the couple. He wanted a curate to stay in his area and suggested delaying job applications in case a job came up in that diocese.

In retrospect the man felt 'so angry'. He lost several months when he might have applied elsewhere and his wife was 'getting desperate' as the summer half-term deadline for giving her notice approached.

He wondered if the incumbent or the bishop could have suggested delaying the move until autumn. Clergy are unfamiliar with the system at the curacy stage, and alternative options may only be seen in retrospect. He saw a future change of job as a 'coming in from the wilderness' experience, even though he had learned so much in two wilderness parishes.

7. Reflections

The interviews showed the all-pervading, emotional, fragmented procedure for clergy families involved in moving. In the previous sections three instances were mentioned of wives being strong and positive despite the uncertainty. Time and again the wives' role was vital in maintaining a precarious family situation with so much at stake.

IV. EDUCATION

Moves were timed as far as possible to fit in with school stages and exams, but the right timing for one child might be difficult for another. Almost without exception the children worried about choosing the right subjects and doing well enough in exams to meet university or career requirements. In inner city and very rural areas the choice of school could be limited and might mean the children travelling considerable distances.

Clergy children had to hold in tension a wide range of imponderables outside their own or the family's control. This included educational reorganization or different systems, which meant additional changes for several families.

1. Choice of school

One family moving to the inner city found there was no vacancy at the local church school. The wife explained the situation to the bishop but it was not mentioned again. Their son spent 20 months at the nearby junior school before moving to the church comprehensive. He was known as Mick the Vic and seen as posh because they lived in a big house and had a second car, a requirement for his mother's job. Equally he was a 'tramp' and was made fun of because he didn't have expensive trainers. 'He's much happier now, more content with lots of friends. At the previous school he seemed to be buying friends and we weren't very happy with a lot of their behaviour.'

Peer pressure is not new. However supportive parents may be, children themselves have to negotiate a place within the local culture.

One wife had a professional link with children at her daughter's school who were taken into care, and they became 'quite clinging' to the daughter. In order to separate from them she chose an alternative senior school, leaving many of her friends behind.

Some choices had unexpected implications. Parents who knew they would move during their daughter's senior school sent her to a Christian boarding school recommended by her head teacher to provide continuity. She was unhappy as a boarder so the family chose a move that would make weekly boarding possible. One of her younger brothers was about to be captain of two sports teams in his final junior year. 'He didn't want to come, said how cruel we were and threatened to run away.' The weekly boarding proved very disruptive, with rush hour journeys at weekends, and the daughter at 14 had no friends in the new village and no contemporaries at church. That family were the first to have children in that village rectory for 50 years. Finally she went to a comprehensive school in a nearby town with just two others from the village in her year. 'It could be because I'm the vicar's daughter that they don't want to make friends with me.' She had a lot of friends in their previous parish so friendships were not a problem generally. The move proved difficult for her parents too who said, 'You cannot foresee all the implications of your decisions'.

2. Public figures

Several clergy were school governors and their families spoke of problems related to being the child of 'so notorious a person as a clergyman'. One couple said the vicar being chair of governors in the only local middle school was not an issue they took into account. They advised their son not to tell everyone but he was quite thrilled that his father was chair. 'Now he wishes he hadn't said anything'. When he was bullied and verbally abused, the son felt he was stupid to be so naïve. 'I just think they're pathetic going on like that. I've got used to it now.' His father thought it had affected his relationship with contemporaries but not the attitude of staff. The son felt the staff once treated him unfairly over bad language and told him off more 'because they expect more of me, and (with a grin) I am a little below average in the behaviour rate! People think vicars' sons are square and posh. Children think that, teachers think that – well, I like heavy metal.'

One son described how a teacher who was a church member had spoken to him at school, saying she'd heard he was badly behaved at the Church Festival supper. New families with young children were joining the congregation and a number of the children caused a disruption. All three clergy children tried to control them, but some older church members found young families hard to cope with and saw the clergy sons as ring-leaders. He already felt unjustly blamed and was livid at the teacher's remarks. The family talked at length about this, and the sense of being watched, reported on and criticised, even on second-hand information. The fact that 'we tried to control them' indicates the strong sense of responsibility shown by all the children.

Another son said yes, other children had parents who were governors 'but a vicar and a governor in the same school . . . I can cope with it just'. At a parents' evening his parents received a monologue from the teacher about herself and the class, 'proving you're doing a good job if there's a governor around'. There was little time left to hear about their son.

A child who was a good athlete with plenty of friends at his previous school said he had 'a lot of stick' when they moved because he was part of a clergy family. He was hit, called names, and mocked, all within the few days before our second interview. He put the intensity at between seven and nine on a scale of ten. He was identified as a clergy child, in spite of not telling his friends, because 'I go into the rectory and go to church on a Sunday morning'.

'As my Dad might be involved in the school round the corner I went to a different senior school', another child said, 'but I lost all my friends of seven years because they all went locally. It's not nice for everybody to know that you're Mr A's daughter.'

3.   Support and 'children sacrificed'

Couples spoke of no one being aware of the difficulties they were facing. One man said there was no more money to pay him when his five-year contract was finished as the funding had been allocated elsewhere. His son had to stay behind for a year to finish his A-levels.

'The decision was made for him'. His new bishop said he had gone through something similar and saw the problem, but nothing more was said.

A country rector felt the stress of leaving things established in a 'missionary situation'. 'We're conscious of the sacrifice our family have had to make. It would be lovely to go to a church with a large youth group for the family and opportunity to do other things they want to do. They have this lovely house to remember and an enormous garden but very few people. It looks good, but living here is difficult for young people. They don't have inner city problems but lead a very extended life with their school an hour away by public transport.'

Another vicar was concerned about the hierarchy's attitude to difficulties for clergy families. He thought his son would find moving traumatic and mentioned this to a senior clergyman, 'who had been a bit of a career priest. I don't think he understood what I was talking about. There was a pause when I said about schooling. He said, "Well, you just have to do these things", whereas it's a prime consideration for us. We've tried to take a hard and honest look at the lives of a lot of senior clergy children and they're all over the place. We're not perfect parents but I worry that a lot of them have been sacrificed.' He had known a variety of clergy families at different stages and levels of ministry through widespread contact in a previous post.

4.   Reflections

When families moved to completely new environments such as rural areas, inner cities or housing estates there were significant cultural adjustments for parents and children alike. Decisions about children's education could then be even more complex. If there had been more opportunity to discuss various options, the families could have made more informed decisions, and above all, felt supported in their isolation.

14 Finance and the Public Role

I. FINANCE

Finance is always an emotive subject and there will always be contrary perspectives to a family's perception of their position. One aim of our research was to provide a forum for the families to be heard and for people to listen to *their* perception. As with other issues there was little sense of complaint about financial difficulties that clergy families faced. They were just relating the situation as they found it.

1. The basic issues

Three basic issues seemed to underlie the question of finance. First, the Double Bind, which operated in various ways for the families, but applied particularly over money. They were asked by the hierarchy to be more independent. Yet in this area, where most people value choice and preference, there was almost no leeway for the families to make independent decisions. Tied accommodation meant that the proportion of their income to be spent on housing had already been decided for them.

Second, the most striking factor of the families' comments about finance was the way clergy viewed their success or failure in terms of the church's giving. If congregations supported special church appeals and paid its quota in full, this was seen as personal affirmation. As our data suggest that clergy are given little general affirmation, this may explain why something so tangible took on such significance. Most clergy worried as much about church finance as they did about their own personal position.

Third, the data showed how damaging it was to the families if comments were made on their financial position by members of their congregation, or indeed by the public. Such comments would almost certainly be based on one or two individual aspects of their situation and not their whole financial position seen in the context of all other aspects of their lives.

A subsidiary issue, brought to light in the interviews, was the considerable support the families received from grandparents, particularly the wife's parents. This included being able to afford holidays, music lessons or sporting activities for their children as well as replacing a car. Again these issues need to be seen in context. They spoke of the difficulty of having holidays at home, the car being essential for the job and how much clergy children should be asked to forego because of a parent's ordination.

2. As time goes by

Several of the families worried about the constant financial pressure, particularly as the children grew older. It seemed one of the couple worried and was depressed about money more than the other. Usually this was the wife, although two men volunteered that they were concerned about money. The fact that his wife was so 'steady and stable and always positive' in another family was itself a pressure for her husband. He felt the responsibility of how the family were going to manage.

Several said that they would not manage financially if their wives did not work. Even with part-time working, one family in a rural parish with four children said that some weeks 'we wonder if we'll make it and then we survive'. Two felt pressurized by the 'knife-edge at the end of the month'. They hated borrowing and applying to charities to get enough money to keep going. One said specifically that it was not really possible to bring up a family on a clergy stipend, and if they were paid more, there would be less stress. This view was confirmed by subsequent comments of the Pastoral Group.

3. Country living

If families were in the country, it was 'immeasurably more difficult' for wives to get a job. The husband could need the car at any time, and public transport was virtually non-existent, so a second car would be necessary even for a part-time job. This was either not viable or meant they would be little better off. Living in the country was seen as more expensive, with almost everything involving a car journey. Heating bills in a large vicarage could be a particular pressure.

There could also be a tension not only between job and family but also between a wife having a job and a sense of commitment to the parish, especially in parishes with few resources and little support. 'Certainly the home, the family and the parish just wouldn't tick so smoothly if Ann were at work.' For another couple in the country her new half-time job 'stretches home life much more than it's ever been stretched before'. They were starting things from scratch in the parish and 'you could put in endless time and be useful'.

4. The children's perception

Most of the children spoke of looking forward to getting a well-paid job and 'having some money for a change'. A son thought that if his father wasn't a clergyman he would earn more money and 'we wouldn't have to row about it. Mum says that even if we did have more, Dad would still scrooge us!' One couple said The Sons of the Clergy charity had enabled them to buy a piano so their musical children could have lessons. For all the difficulties, an 11-year-old saw a positive aspect. 'We're pretty well off because we're a family and as long as we can manage it's much better to be all right than in debt all the time like everybody else'.

5. Finance and stress

The sense of pressure the families felt over finance is evident. One teenage daughter spelt out how stress itself could specifically affect their financial position. She said that when her father was under pressure he was more likely to spend money on his credit card, often on the family, creating the additional pressure of how they would make ends meet when the reckoning came. This was interesting in terms of the bishops' concern about high credit card debt.

Another concern was how the family would manage if the wife's job came to an end. There was also the question of whether the wife would get another job if they moved. Given the families' comments, this could be crucial.

6. Public perception and family help

The public perception of the families' situation was frequently guided by what people saw. 'There's very little concept from local people of the pressure. The image is that "they're doing very nicely, thank you". You live in a big house and have a nice car but the car is only because of my wife's family'. Another family said parishioners tended to make remarks 'because they don't believe us, and don't think we're badly paid. They're very conscious that we have a house provided. One or two are very aware, but most think that if clergy were paid less they wouldn't have to pay so much quota. Very difficult when you sit at PCC meetings and they say, 'Why do we have to pay so much quota?' He thought they really meant 'Why do we have to pay the clergy so much?'

We have seen how important holidays were to the families because of limited time together during the rest of the year. If the wife's family didn't pay for it, one family with small children said they wouldn't have a holiday. Another couple with a baby and a toddler cancelled two weeks at her parents' when her sister moved back home. 'People couldn't understand why we couldn't go away and we couldn't explain it. The only way we can go to my parents is that the petrol's paid for by the food we save.' They stayed at home for that holiday and had a very interrupted time. This couple came from a home parish that usually paid for the vicar's annual holiday. Such a discrepancy in support may add to the public's misperception of clergy family finance.

One vicar had received no expenses for that year. Even though it was a financial embarrassment to them as a family, he would not consider raising it, as he thought those responsible would then be embarrassed. It should have been paid quarterly in advance but he thought it was probably carelessness rather than deliberate neglect. He knew the problem would be rectified at the end of the financial year as 'parishes are obliged by the archdeacon to record how much they've paid, so that actually protects the clergy from an ongoing situation.'

A clergy wife was not consulted when churchwardens and a small group decided that she should not be paid for playing the organ, although all previous organists had been paid. She felt exploited. Later she was told that only one voice had been raised against payment but this had carried the day. As with curate's housing this raises questions about how decisions, which may significantly affect clergy and their families, are made within a church.

7.   Personalized finance

One incumbent struggled to explain his situation. There were few professional people in the parish to give support, both practical and professional, so the only support came from his wife. 'The deanery chapter, rural dean, archdeacon and the bishop agree that there is need for help but nothing happens. I don't think we'll get a curate till we can pay our quota in full. I can understand the diocese saying they won't pour good money after bad. I believe that's false thinking but the rural dean has suggested that the quota *is* a factor. The deanery and diocese should be sufficiently mission oriented to subsidize an adequate ministry here, both financially and in other ways'.

In the last interview, two years later, he said that the diocesan authorities had few ways of measuring what is happening in any congregation or parish. 'I believe our ability to pay the quota affects how people in the diocese and the deanery view my ministry. I find it a difficult pressure to face continually. Our giving has increased but the quota increase makes it seem that we are not moving forward. I'm not necessarily responsible for solving it on my own but I am responsible for leadership here. At the level of thinking it through, it's stress.'

His wife did not think parishioners saw it in those terms. 'They are not going to see it as an assessment of what I'm doing here, no, but it's not easy to make them aware of the seriousness of the situation. They'd be shocked if deanery changes meant there was no vicar here.' That diocese, among others, had talked about deducting shortfall from minister's stipends and this vicar would have lost £5,000 a year. Not only was the incumbent personalizing the church's financial situation but so were sections of the diocese.

On the other hand if he were given a curate, he felt it would look as though the diocese was 'pouring in all these extra resources' and that would 'increase the pressure to produce the goods here'. So either way, there would be pressure and he would still not know why the curate had come. Was it how the diocese viewed his ministry, or because the diocese and deanery had become more 'mission oriented', or that they appreciated the increased giving by the parish even though the quota had not been met?

Another vicar described a convoluted situation in a country parish. He was concerned that quotas went on rising. 'We're taking in a fifth parish next year which will help us financially but knock us back pastorally, as we'll have to find more people to run services and set up an infrastructure. The £6,000 quota they will contribute will help us enormously. I could be very cynical and say that returning the patronage to the local patron (rather than the bishop) if we take another parish has been a bit of blackmail. However, despite reduced financial pressure, the vicar personally would bear the brunt of a greater workload in a parish he had just described as 'absolutely stretched'.

A recently-installed vicar spoke of worry about money at the church and how he would like to see it financially sound. The church was a Grade 1 listed building which was 'a ball and chain financially'. They were considering involving the town in raising money for upkeep.

A couple who had struggled on a difficult estate said in the third interview that they felt more settled. There wasn't any one thing in particular that had contributed to this. There had been a lot of adjustment for the wife in particular, another instance of leaving her job and having children in an isolated situation. Antagonism to the previous vicar had also left an atmosphere of tension but 'the other factor in feeling more settled has been knowing that we're liked. People in the churches like us *and the response to the roof appeal has shown that*'.

8. Reflections

The data show that the boundaries between personal and professional issues in the realm of finance were significantly blurred. Various financial choices were dictated by the size of house and its location, the type of area and access to services and facilities that went with particular jobs. Limited stipends meant there was no potential increase to anticipate as children's needs grew and extra finance would not be there to compensate for long hours as in other professions. Nevertheless, the public often judged the financial position of clergy on appearances, which might be quite unrelated to their actual situation.

Church giving was often seen by clergy as a very personal responsibility, especially in areas where congregations struggled to meet the quota. Most of them spoke of worry over various aspects of church finance. Some judged their performance or personal popularity on the level of giving, or feared that staff at diocesan level viewed it in this way. Upkeep of church buildings was also a heavy burden that was not always shared. During all the discussions relating to finance, the commitment of the couples to the parish with its many demands was clearly evident. Some wives worked shorter hours to prepare and be available for special events, like a parish fete in their

garden, or to contribute to the overall tasks of the parish. Children were very aware, as in other aspects of their lives, that life would have been very different if their parents had still been working in their previous professions.

With previous experience and moves the 20 families had held appointments in almost half of the 42 dioceses, so the research was able to draw on this considerable breadth of experience.

II. THE PUBLIC ROLE

In Chapter 4 we explored the effects on families of one member being in the public eye and Janet Finch's suggestion that clergy families are 'seen as public figures (and role models) essentially defined in terms of work for the purposes of almost all social contacts'. Once clergy and their families are in the vicarage or rectory, their public role comes much more to the fore. Our research families anticipated being seen as primary representatives of the Christian faith in their community, but quickly realized the widespread and often unexpected impact of their position on relationships generally. They never knew when the public or the congregation might have a particular agenda or set of expectations in mind. The family's motives or actions then could so easily be misconstrued or offence given. They realized too, as we saw for local elected councillors, that the press or pressure groups might use them as spokespeople or examples over a range of issues.

1. The Panopticon

An interesting example of how people react when they never know if they are being watched is the Panopticon, designed by Jeremy Bentham. This is a circular construction one room deep, lit in such a way that guards in a central watchtower can see the prisoners in each cell but cannot be seen themselves. The prisoners therefore never know if the guards are there. In time they behave as though they are being watched all the time. Strangeways Prison is a classic example.

There were a number of instances in the interviews when the families showed this sense of being in the public eye, as well as the many comments from the children. A minor traffic accident caused by a clergyman was reported in the local press leaving him with a sense of exposure. 'One of the problems of being well known in a community of this sort and size is that people notice it's "The Rev …". People know I don't drink so there'd be no suspicion that I'd been drinking.' His son was more pragmatic. 'Everyone doesn't know that who reads the paper.'

Another son asked his father to practise goal-keeping with him on ground being claimed by the local rugby club. The vicar saw the danger of being caught in the dispute. 'It would be all right if I'd been Joe Bloggs of Barn Lane, but I was conscious that people know who I am. If that was the week the club chose to clamp down, they could cause a rumpus' or it could hit the headlines.

2. The vicarage family

Couples were conscious that the whole family became the focus of expectations and sometimes of criticism. They spoke of how hard it could be to distinguish between criticism you can shrug off and criticism to which you have to pay attention. It was particularly difficult to shrug off criticism of their children or even to know how to deal with it.

A father whose children had experienced verbal attacks from adults and contemporaries said they were under pressure and stress because of their position at the centre of things. After one particularly difficult episode his son told his father to change his job. 'It must have hurt him quite a lot and afterwards I felt sorry.' His father had forgotten about the incident and said it was still quite difficult to hear of it now. He had in fact spoken to the adult concerned – and they hadn't moved.

Two brothers said that older people in the congregation expected them to be perfect. When they were criticised, their father said he tended to leave the situation, although normally he dealt with problems as they arose. He felt like a sponge, taking in lots of hurt because they were singled out in a very unfair way. If he made an issue of it, his children could become the centre of controversy, 'so I just grin and bear it'.

The boys said they were teased a lot for being the vicar's children, and living in the big house, which 'you don't have to pay for 'cos your Dad's the vicar'. The older one said the teasing made him very irritable and he 'took it out' on his younger brother so the stress was passed on.

It could be passed on, too, from clergy to their children. 'Stress creates emotional disturbance in me and then I can't always differentiate between the need to discipline the children and the other emotions that I'm carting around. There can be a very direct route between the two. That's why I say they are victims. The thing they often contribute to the situation is humour.'

Working from home was an added complication as personal and professional boundaries became confused. A vicar with young children said, 'I can hear what is happening in the rest of the house from my study. If I hear my wife struggling I can't stay there and ignore it. I just don't know how to deal with that.'

People compared clergy children with their own and used them as a benchmark. 'Comparisons are constantly made with ours. We get a tremendous amount of it, probably because we're a public family, seen as being slightly different. We don't enter into this. It's a case of doing ours down in order to raise theirs up.' Another spoke of the children being set up on pedestals. 'You need to counter those things by not taking yourself or their expectations too seriously. They're totally unrealistic and unhealthy. That's the road to breakdown.'

It could be difficult to 'shrug off' even far-fetched criticism if its source and extent were unknown. A churchwarden told a vicar's wife with three small children that 'someone had said' she wasn't seen often enough and should push the pram round each village once a week. She didn't know who had said it or why. Then a man, whose wife went to church once a month, told her he expected her to be at both churches every week. One rule for clergy families, she felt, another for members.

A couple with very young children said their parish 'could do with someone staying much longer than the five- or seven-year contract of a team vicar's post, but most people wouldn't want to come here for more. It needs time to build up trust because clergy tend to be different from local people so the process is quite slow.' The husband added, 'I wouldn't want my children to grow up here. I just wouldn't'. Their daughter had found the rough treatment she had in playgroup and nursery quite frightening.

The clergy commented on the centrality of their wife's support and the importance of the family. One priest said they looked on the job as a family commitment. He knew very well that he could not fulfil his calling without the family. Yet the effect of a demanding area and pressure on the family needed to be monitored. Another priest said he would have to resign if his wife died, as he would not feel able to go on without her.

Their public role could make it hard to ask for support because of the family's position. One vicar had been under great pressure and saw the anxiety in his wife's face. He thought she was aware of the high expectation people had of him, so if he found it hard to cope, there might be two possible reactions. People might lose their respect for him, or they might think if he couldn't cope, how could they possibly cope themselves. The question of loyalty meant she found it difficult to share her worry about him with anybody else. So she was left to carry her anxiety.

The pressures led another to say he could see a considerable argument to support a non-married priesthood, 'not because it's better but because of the strain the parochial ministry puts on the family and the demands it makes on an individual. I think we've got the message wrong. You can't have two priorities of equal standing. You've got to say one's first and the other's second. The first people in my life are my family and the parish now has to be second fiddle'. The reality proved otherwise.

3. The supporting cast and protection

If clergy spouses were in the house they could be caught up in a whole variety of unexpected requests at a moment's notice. The wives said how difficult and time-consuming they found it to be treated as parish assistants, frequently expected to know what their husbands were doing or where they were going by 'all sorts of people, members, non-members, funeral directors'. They mentioned being asked to let workmen, gasmen, organ tuners into church, funerals in and out of burial grounds or people into the churchyard to see a grave, even at lunchtime on Christmas Day!

Children were inducted into the helping role from an early age. One ten-year-old said he hated all the fetching and carrying he had to do at church. Later his father said he was pleased that 'Jack enjoys doing things in church, being an apprentice vicar, apprentice churchwarden, apprentice PA man, music group member ...'. Other parents valued the uncomplaining way their children helped to take materials for Sunday school and services to the church some distance away. When one vicar asked children to come to the front of the church, his three-year-old, sitting near the front anyway, announced, "*I'm* the church boy", as though this was his role. His parents were amazed not only that he said it but that he had thought it in the first place.

Children hated that 'everything's a rush at weekends'; fathers taking services and talking to people, mothers, even with quite small children, playing the organ, running Sunday schools, crèches and youth groups, entertaining visiting speakers or parishioners and having very little space for themselves and the family. One wife spoke of weekends as stepping on a treadmill. Some church members expressed support and understanding but still left the wives to cope, and wondered how they managed. Another said it would be nice to have a normal weekend. 'You forget what it was like to finish work on Friday night and go back on Monday morning.'

Sometimes members of the congregation would press for events such as Mothers' Union functions, flower festivals, or fetes to be in the vicarage garden, and promise to help. When the time came they would be on holiday or 'busy with their own gardens', leaving clergy wives to cope. One found herself running the harvest supper on her own when all the committee dropped out. When 'help didn't materialize for the fete', another gardened at 6 am each morning for several weeks and took time off work. 'You could go to the extreme and not do anything but then everyone would say, "Good heavens. Look what they've done to the garden". It's silly really. Maybe you should just leave it but . . . The following year we said it would be in the church hall. It was a damp day but I still heard people say, "Why isn't it in the garden?" ' A teenager's remark showed parishioners were in fact watching and commenting. 'A lady came round just as we got back from holiday and said, "Your garden looks a bit of a mess, I thought I'd tidy it up for you". OK it's very nice of her but it's a bit of a cheek when she thinks that it's like cleaning the church.'

The sense that the vicarage and garden were part of the church was hard to contend with especially if there was no church hall. 'It's not public property for everybody. I am accessible but I still want to make it very clear that it's our home. The children said, 'We were eating outside one day when two old ladies who'd been walking on the common appeared. "Oh, we're sorry, we can't go all the way round so we thought we'd just pop through your garden" '.

The families' comments were echoed in an article in the *Church Times* on 25 February, 2005, on behalf of Save our Parsonages, speaking of the many potential uses of larger vicarages. 'They can offer opportunities to bring the church back into the centre of community life and in rural areas can be a hub of village activity and may touch the lives of people who might never consider going to church. Many vicarage dining rooms have been commandeered for the production of parish magazines. Meetings of churchwardens may spill into the larger reception rooms, while a parsonage next to the church can give a suitable setting for a Sunday school, Bible study groups, Mothers' Union meetings, and confirmation classes . . . at the invitation of the incumbent. In spite of such valuable outreach, some dioceses are reluctant to recognize the parsonage as a public building'. Given the inter-related issues of security for the family, expectations, criticism and privacy, Archdeacon John Cox's firm reply in the same edition that the parsonage is not primarily a public place may need to be emphasized more strongly.

This issue of intrusion caused real concern to families with children of all ages because their house was so public. One wife said, 'opening the door is like opening up the family'. She was conscious of how the children were behaving but was also 'like a lioness looking after her young' because of the sort of callers who came. Another said that when her son was very young, a girl would regularly come to the house after taking overdoses. He was in the midst of it and experienced 'things which you would not want your children to experience'.

The parents were wary of leaving their children alone in the house even at 13 and 14. One young teenager said he liked his Dad to be there. 'We get these people, some are schizophrenic, some drunk, one came yesterday saying there was "something in their house". It was late in the evening when Dad went with him and we got really, really worried.' A nine-year-old said drunks or tramps came round to the back of the house and it was really dangerous. Most vicarages stood on their own so the children's anxieties were understandable.

4. Ennui and support

The endless routine could produce what one couple described as 'the five year flump'. 'There's an oppressive feeling around and you wonder if you'll ever get anywhere. The calendar looms up with the harvest coming along *again* and we wonder if we can cope with just going on and on. Things don't seem to be progressing much and you seem to be doing the same thing. The children's summer clubs have dwindled a bit and we're not seeing the families being drawn into the life of the church. You think, do I do it next year?' The Leadership Group were concerned at the ennui many clergy faced in their 50s, but this priest was under 45.

Without support this ennui might well slide into depression. The clergy had said how infrequent their contacts were with bishops and archdeacons, so we noted each time any contact was mentioned in the interviews. We were struck by how few there were.

A couple in the inner city spoke very strongly about lack of support. 'Bishops and the diocese don't have a *clue* about ministry in the inner city. I think it's appalling that we had to buy our own security lights in an area like this. Their attitude certainly increases the stress. If they really understood how to get close to local people they wouldn't put us in a big house like this'. He had come close to resigning over minimum support and interest from the diocese both to them as a church and as a family.

One man under particular pressure said his bishop had been supportive of his saying 'No' to more things in his parish but you couldn't say 'No' to everything. The one organizational issue that would have reduced the stress, the bishop refused to allow for financial reasons.

5. Reflections

Parish ministry could be 'enormously fulfilling', and much love and concern could be given to clergy families. One family spoke of being 'given a lot of love' that would otherwise have come from extended family.

On the other side, the ongoing strain for all members of clergy families from being the focus of expectations and public attention had many facets. Clergy homes and gardens were often seen as public property and privacy was not always respected.

Parents were concerned at the risk posed to all family members having to deal with the public, including those with mental health problems, sometimes on their own in an isolated house. Protecting children from unfair criticism could risk a backlash. Parishioners could impose significant burdens on clergy families by initially supporting particular events and opting out when the time came. Lack of support from the diocese was expressed not only in terms of practical help but also in lack of understanding.

Attempting to balance the ideal of the public image in both the job and the family left clergy couples in a Double Bind. They wanted to put their families first, but they accommodated to the situation by putting the job first, with the family drawn into the heart of the task. If the accumulated stress leads to loss of motivation, boredom, breakdown or inappropriate behaviour, these reactions too would be in the public domain.

15 The Clergy View of the Job and its Impact on the Family; and Days Off

I.   THE JOB AND THE FAMILY

1.   The vision and the task

Two particular issues stood out as the clergy described the many aspects of their job. One was the lack of opportunity to think through their plans and decisions with other clergy or supervisors, and in some cases with lay leaders. The other was the central role played by their spouses in terms of support and encouragement.

The clergy were very conscious of the enormity of the task with all its facets, and anxious about their ability to meet its demands. They spoke of their lack of time, energy and ongoing creativity. 'I recognize that the job of a clergyman is simply much more than a job', one man commented. 'Remaining open to what God wants of us, in the midst of everything else that is happening, is something that involves constant practice and often considerable failure because I don't consistently do that.' Another struggled with how he would know what God wanted him to do. 'You work on a feeling and check it out with other people. If that's done prayerfully and sensitively then that is as much as one can be sure, say 80 per cent in the end.'

The clergy looked to develop their own and others' leadership skills and anticipated growth in numbers, spiritual depth and commitment. One priest expressed the overall sense that developing spiritual depth in the congregation is a basic aim for clergy. Another aim was to help members lose their 'fortress mentality' and share their faith with greater confidence. They were convinced that their own spirituality was central to the task, 'that is the key and part of the answer to how you get the parish to grow. They are inter-related not separate'.

They were also concerned about deciding on priorities in their work. 'If I didn't go out visiting for three months or went every day, nobody would know because only a limited number of people are seeing it. It's the official things that people notice. If I missed church council meetings or didn't prepare sermons they'd notice pretty quickly because preaching is quite important here and I'd have no new material, no stimulus. It's the sort of place where people expect things to happen, not just to drift along. It's something I like but it does take a lot of work.' The vicar who found these tasks were squeezed out said, 'I read less and less and I'm more and more busy. I get so behind with all sorts of things.'

One priest, ordained for 20 years, commented on the year he had described during the interview. 'When I look at it on the flip chart it seems horrific. Everything my year's been to me has been to do with my work. It says nothing about me personally. Very sad really!'

Another said, 'Seeing it all down on paper, I'm amazed by the amount that has happened.' If he had not realized it himself because there was no one to tell, who else would have noticed? He thought possibly his curate.

Clergy involvement in diocesan activities may not be seen or understood by the parish, but time had to be found for this extra demand. Two of the clergy were rural deans. One vicar had written a paper for the diocese on different denominations working together while he was ill in bed. He said the hierarchy saw the outcome as 'an enormous success'. They would not have known he had written it during an illness. Parishioners would probably have known nothing at all about the time and preparation that was involved.

2. A joint responsibility – working in partnership with the laity

Most of our research clergy spoke of the importance of being open to God and of involving others in planning, rather than deciding on a course of action and imposing it. 'So far I have shared my vision with my wife and we have prayed it through together. Now we must share it with the people who know the parish, get feedback and prayerfully test if this is what God wants. Some of our thoughts would absolutely petrify them so it has to be done gently with loving care.'

152 ◆ *Public People, Private Lives*

Not all parishes had a strong nucleus of lay people with whom the incumbent could discuss his thoughts. One priest in his first very run-down parish said, 'I feel very inadequate when I look at the development and growth we need and then at the people we've got. The two are incompatible. Have I got the gifts and skills to deal with it? I just have to say, "Don't worry, God's in control. When things are right they'll happen".' Who would give him support? 'There's potential to discuss the situation with some clergy who I relate to. The danger of talking to clergy is that they tell you not to worry. I want someone who will just let me say it.'

Another was disillusioned with lay leaders when two Diocesan representatives came to meet each PCC in his parish about a campaign. 'At one PCC no one was there except the couple hosting it. I was disappointed and embarrassed. The churchwardens sent apologies but no one has since mentioned it. The veil of silence is very difficult and may shorten my stay here.' This was one of many instances that showed the importance of good communication between members and the clergy. A wife said, 'In our home church people made lots of comments on services and sermons. Here you get no feedback and little encouragement. I guess he gets his encourage-ment from his calling, how things are going at a particular time, and from his innovations. We've had to adjust to it.'

Another issue that several clergy mentioned was the long-term effects of a difficult incumbency and the time taken to re-establish a clergy and lay team. 'The last team rector didn't have a very happy time here. There was friction with parish members. A lot of people were very hurt and some left the church. The team fragmented. There was a two-year interregnum and a full review. It will be good to see growth and new projects develop again in the next few years. But the present lay leadership are unwilling to move forward spiritually. They don't want anything to change. They're not fighting you but have no enthusiasm to go along with you. Newer members are not in positions of leadership yet.' Who would give him support at this point? He felt this would come from the present team, a real advantage of teamwork.

In another church the previous vicar had quadrupled his congregation and then left with someone else's wife. The new incumbent was still compared with him and expected to produce 1,001 ideas like he had. In fact, he was having to handle the legacy of mistrust left by that vicar's behaviour, and also trying to unite two congregations, one charismatic, one traditional. Comparison with predecessors was made in various ways. One priest had enjoyed meeting parishioners in the pub, but this was not the present vicar's scene.

A vicar in the inner city realized from the start that his parish was not what it had seemed at interview. Lay leaders were unreliable. He felt disappointed and let down. 'I came here on a ticket of shared ministry with lay ministry teams, but for 60 per cent of my time I'm an administrator, dealing with buildings and money, and helping people to cope with each other. Things I felt gifted for just haven't happened. Lay people said they couldn't do visiting again because they'd done it in the past and I'd "do it properly because I was the ordained man". At times I resent it.'

This idea of 'he'll do it properly because he is the ordained person' comes in many guises and suggests that church members and members of the public may see clergy as 'Electric Monks'. Adams[1] describes the Electric Monk as 'a labour-saving device, like a dishwasher or a video recorder. Dishwashers wash tedious dishes for you, saving you the bother of washing them yourself; video recorders watch tedious television for you, saving you the bother of looking at it yourself. Electric Monks believe things for you, thus saving you what was becoming an increasingly onerous task, that of believing all the things the world expected you to believe'. Members may attempt to use clergy, or their families, as Electric Monks in terms of Christian belief and sharing faith with others. If so, this prevents faith and the Church's mission being worked through together as a joint responsibility.

3. The diversity of the job

The complexity of some parishes brought particular pressures. A new incumbent was rescuing 'the old city centre church from closure and giving it a new purpose involving the political and the controversial'. A separate task was to build a traditional worshipping community in his second church. With 'two totally different set-ups' he was concerned that the job was too big for one person. 'Lack of time produces stress and I start going round in circles. I have to keep that sorted and when necessary turn my back on it.'

---

1   Adams, D. (1988) *Dirk Gently's Holistic Detective Agency*. London: Pan Books.

Another felt the stress of balancing his four parishes, 'not letting the ones that are going badly bring you down, and being encouraged by the folk on an up – the advantage of more than one church.'

Judging the right pace for making changes was often a challenge and pressure. The crisis with his churchwarden was a time of great anxiety for one vicar but he'd learned from it. Consequently, he had handled a further problem quite differently. Another said, 'Changing churchwardens was done brutally and firmly by me, adding to bad feeling at the time but this vanished very quickly. It has opened up parish life immensely.'

Growth brought great encouragement as well as pressure. The growing togetherness of one priest's parish was, he said, very marked. Another 'put in a third tier of worship' as current services were full, but this reduced rehearsal time for the choir and for other jobs. The issues had 'taken far more emotional energy than they need.'

Energy, both physical and emotional, was a factor that worried the clergy even in this 30– 45 age group. 'I'm only in my early 40s,' a new incumbent said, 'but it's quite old for some of the things I want to do.' He was concerned too about expectations from one of his congregations whose approach he described as 'this very charismatic rushing around'.

Creativity was a similar but different concern. 'In my last job my creativity was waning after five years. So much depends on your still being creative, having a vision for the place, and being able to keep things fresh and alive. How could I be here for another two years if I felt I'd nothing to offer? Yet I need to stay because I can't destabilize the family.' His wife had another perspective: 'It's your assumption that everything pivots around your creativity. It might do this lot good if they had to be more creative themselves'. Their teenage son spoke with considerable insight, 'It's Dad's job satisfaction though, isn't it?' His older brother saw the other side of the coin: 'Dad sets too high standards for himself'.

One man questioned his pattern of working after attending a course. 'It made me realize I was trying to deal with everything myself, and not allowing the management structure to manage the parish. I certainly felt locked in a treadmill. I wasn't free to be creative and make proactive rather than reactive decisions, and there was no room for me to think about myself. The course, with the rigorous analysis of the parish I had to do first, was the most significant thing I've done for years. I've got a new sense of working towards something. I'm looking forward to using the course in whatever I do next.'

The analysis he had done also made him think about the family's position. 'On my diagram of the parish and the family I thought you, as a family, probably saw yourselves figuring way outside all my work but that isn't how it feels. I have an idealized view that everything here at home can be kept away from all that is going on out there, but I know it can't be separate. Half our life is there, in the work area, whether we like it or not because it can't be divorced from my work. It overlaps.' Work consultancy led another man to take a supervision course and learn new management skills. 'That course changed my behaviour with churchwardens and with my Reader. I'm much firmer in dealing with things and not letting them go.' These courses linked with many of the job issues discussed generally by the research clergy. They were demanding but seen as positive and giving participants new confidence for the task. Only two other clergy mentioned a similar course or work consultancy. Without this opportunity to gain a wider perspective they were left to carry the weight of such diverse responsibility. 'Part of the pressure is feeling responsible for keeping the show on the road and actually hurting if things don't go well.' Another looked at all the demands of the next few years and said, 'I feel a certain deepness in my spirit whenever I think of it'.

Prayer and the support of their wives were central to the clergy but in professional terms there was an overall sense throughout of coping alone. A rural vicar said their main support came from 'seeing some very close friends every half term who understand what we're about. There's the stress on us of wanting to leave things established, and sometimes just wanting to leave! It would be great to go to a church with a large youth group for our family.'

Another felt the team provided opportunities to share the pressures of work and to reflect on the job with them rather than at home. 'I don't want to load my wife up with my angst from work. We've shared our feelings a lot about being here but haven't analysed between us the underlying cause of our frustration and anger.' The team was providing some support but the difficulties of a very tough area were still causing pressure in the family.

4. Going on going on

The Leadership Group spoke of the problem of ennui, especially for those working in isolated situations like rural or inner city areas or enclosed estates. Three comments illustrate the dilemma.

'A few months ago I found myself with a bit of a crisis thinking, "Where am I going?" I'm at a point in life when I haven't got ambitions beyond being in the sort of situation I'm in now, with a family and a house like we have, but I can't envisage years and years more of the same. I have ambitions to serve God where I am but not to go up in any diocesan hierarchy.'

Another priest who spoke of finding parish ministry enormously fulfilling said,

'I don't have any targets beyond doing my job better. I can't imagine doing a different job but I need a change now from the kind of urban ministry I've been involved in for the past ten years, otherwise I'll be stuck in it. Another 30 years of it would kill me. In fact a lot less would kill me. With so many years ahead of me I think I could take time out in a non-parochial post. The future doesn't feel frightening but quite exciting both staying here and going. A year ago I would just have wanted to go.'

Much else that this family said showed how the pressures of inner city life had almost led to a crisis in family relationships. The family had carried the stress alone, with only one sign, evident to the hierarchy several years earlier, of the cost of coping in that sort of area.

Would the hierarchy have allowed this particular priest to 'be stuck in urban ministry'? Many comments from the families suggested that one way to combat lack of stimulation and the ensuing ennui was to have a variation in types of parish. Although clergy might develop expertise in working in particular areas, the hierarchy may need to consider whether a *family* should live in a second or even a third 'difficult area'.

A third clergyman said,

'I'm fairly laid back. It certainly helps as a priest, otherwise one would be a nervous wreck. It's circular. The more one is laid back the more one goes on in ministry. I think it's true of most clergy I know.'

5. Organizational issues

Many times the clergy spoke of schemes being set up on a basis of expediency rather than being properly planned, leaving clergy to overcome organizational difficulties that were the responsibility of the diocese.

One man said no one planned his new post. 'The bishop set it up quickly without thinking it through. I was there, the need was there, and the two things came together.' Suitable accommodation had not been found so two families and the man himself bore the brunt of poor organization.

Another looked back at the 'wonderfully vague correspondence about a complicated scheme for team ministry' set up by the bishop. 'Only after talking at length to the churchwardens did I discover what was behind the written word of the job description rather than what bishops or rectors had hinted at. You really don't know what you're letting yourself in for till you're there.'

A team vicar had had a seven-year contract, 'except there wasn't a contract! The team rector is already past his seven years. Nobody knows what to do, so we're setting up a meeting next month.' How had the meeting come about? His comments to the Reader made her suddenly realize that she, as a lay person, might be running the parish within 18 months, as all the clergy could leave in the same year. She then nagged the team rector. Why wasn't this done at a normal staff meeting? 'It just doesn't happen like that'.

Unclear boundaries and procedures in Local Ecumenical Projects (LEPs) were also highlighted. One new team vicar spoke of changes in his LEP. 'Before I had a chance to touch base, the goal posts were moving. There was a confusion of authority. The Free Church minister is my colleague, my partner, not my junior, but *I* was being asked to make decisions. So far we've got on fine but if there were a dispute, how would we find a solution without an arbiter? It isn't really the function of the Local Advisory Group (which monitors projects) although if it was really serious it might have to go there'.

An inner city parish was asked to have a formal sharing agreement with a nearby Baptist congregation whose minister had left. There was no proper planning. Most of the Baptist members came from outside the parish and had a more fundamentalist outlook. They also had further education in contrast to local people. The vicar believed very strongly that he should serve the needs of the area and found this group very demanding. 'It's beginning to feel like a cuckoo's egg. They make a lot of noise but don't actually deliver. They always have something else to do.'

6. Reflections

The sense of professional isolation that the clergy described was often all-pervasive and, as their discussions show, their main support came from their spouses. Throughout the discussions there was an overriding sense that work consultancy once or twice a year, and ongoing supervision/consultation on a regular basis, could make a great difference to the incumbent's whole professional context. This support could reduce pressure and uncertainty in all the variety of complications and tricky decisions the clergy faced. Regular supervision would also provide continuity of thinking and set current dilemmas in the wider perspective of overall goals for the parish, the growth in numbers, spiritual depth and commitment.

Ongoing training for clergy seemed to transform the way they handled the many complex aspects of the job, and increased their confidence and sense of purpose. One priest was completing an MPhil but only three other clergy spoke of courses rather than day conferences or workshops, although we discussed the whole period of their ministry. Continuing professional development is now emphasized and is often obligatory for ongoing registration and professional recognition in most professions.

The lack of ongoing training and stimulation for clergy may link to the Leadership Group's concern about the problem of clergy suffering from ennui. A priest also suggested that clergy being laid back was 'the only way of coping with the job'. This could leave the hierarchy with the dilemma of not knowing if a priest was being laid back or suffering from ennui, or whether they were different aspects of the same thing. Both consultation and ongoing training could address this.

The Leadership Group's proactive suggestion that there should be a 'day-to-day safety net and monitoring how *families* are handling 'difficult areas' could also address ennui. It would enable the families to discuss the issues they face during a year in a natural way, without seeming to complain, and provide a safeguard against potential breakdown of health, mental health or marriage.

Two comments about staffing of 'difficult areas' were significant. First, a couple working in a team raised the issue that 'slightly broken people' looking for jobs, say, after a breakdown, could have problems getting 'the nicer jobs'. 'Parishes don't want to take a risk, so these (broken) people end up as team vicars in difficult estate situations that are hard to fill.' Given what couples working in that sort of environment said about pressure and isolation, this could create a double vulnerability. Appointments to these areas may need to be carefully monitored at the time of application as well as during an incumbency. Second, the Leadership Group spoke of evangelical couples being more willing to go to difficult areas and less likely to complain, suggesting their idealism in turn could make them vulnerable.

II. DAYS OFF

In our discussion on curates' days off in Chapter 6 III, we showed how the idea of 'leave' indicated not only 'on vacation' but also 'not at work', providing a much clearer sense of a boundary between work and leisure. Lay church members may spend their 'leave' at weekends involved in church activities, in contrast to their normal employment. The boundary between work and leisure is denied if clergy are involved in church activities on their day off, as they are not 'on leave' from their daily work.

It may be important, too, to remember that comments from the families were often in the context of the parents having had secular jobs before ordination with experience of a variety of work environments.

The families felt there was so much to be packed into a day off that it was difficult to relax and hard to be off duty if they spent that day at home. Sometimes they felt obliged to go to a church member's funeral or external meeting. The parents tried to balance a constant tension between personal time and time for the family as a whole, including wider family, especially older parents. One striking finding from the analysis was that hardly any hobbies or personal interests were mentioned.

1. The difficulty of relaxing

Three of the men said they worked a three-shift day and most implied this. They spoke of 'the all-embracing nature of the job' or 'ending up working all hours'. A wife who had worked in industry dubbed it the ultimate in flexi time with no parameters. As Handy pointed out in the Doughnut Principle in Chapter 12, for clergy 'there is no limit to their responsibilities'.

One man said how the feeling of having to work so hard all the time affected his family. 'You think about your sermon in the bath or shower, you think about your service as you get dressed, you think about what you have to do and how you'll handle some situation, all while you're dealing with your family. So they lose out.' He wondered if he would be the same if he was still an executive but his wife said, 'You'd be coming home'. 'Right', he said, 'So there'd be a boundary'.

The pace of work made it very difficult to relax. One man said 'I'm a very conscientious person and from the moment I was ordained I have thrown my whole self into work. Consequently relaxation has become a low priority, squeezed out of every aspect of our lives. So I find days off extremely difficult. Not because I don't like them. I do, and on the whole I take them.' Several said the lack of space meant that they had too high an expectation of a day off 'because it is just one day' and they tried to pack too much into it. They implied that they only found space when it was too late and they were exhausted. This brought its own pressure and some spoke of 'ending up doing very little' that day.

A teenage son put another angle on the need for space. He thought Dad liked being on his own. 'Being with people all the time is pretty stressful. Some people may travel to work and be on their own in the car. For him, not having to travel and being with the family, he's always with someone, all the time.' He felt his father was at his best after very occasionally getting away for a long walk.

2. Interruptions to days off

Most found it difficult to have days off at home because it was hard to be unavailable. A couple in a village did not get that many interruptions but at the back of their minds there was always the possibility of people calling about, for example, baptisms, marriages, funerals. 'Most people expect you to be available for them and a distorted rumour would soon get round the village that you wouldn't see them. The local police used to put CLOSED on the door. It would be nice to do that but people would interpret it as a bad witness.'

One man said that he never answered the phone on his day off because he had often been caught up in something complicated that could have waited. He still found himself going into the study to look for messages. 'It's ridiculous but I did it again last week. I don't find the areas where work touches my home life particularly easy. We get on with it because we've got used to it'. The contradictions in this section are obvious. They accommodated to the situation.

Families with working wives and school-age children frequently found a mismatch between their time off at weekends and the clergy day off in the week. One man had never seen a clergyman who actually managed to take Saturdays off in practice. It was hard to have everything prepared for Sunday by Friday evening. Also most lay people were freer on a Saturday so church activities were tailored to that. The son of a vicar who tried to take Saturdays off resented that the curate had more Saturdays off than his father.

3. Conflicting expectations

Each member of the family saw official invitations differently. Wives might feel they should go to parish weddings or parties even on days off. Clergy might be 'in a corner with someone talking about work' but feel guilty about taking alternative time off. 'I can't say "I cannot attend this meeting because it's important to have time with my family". Parishioners are often in the same position so we don't make a big thing of clergy days off in church. A few weeks ago somebody said, "Well I don't get a day off at all", so it does tend to niggle a bit. There are people who are over-committed both at work and at church and I haven't the heart to labour it too much'. Supervision/consultation could help clergy to realize the damage of such diffuse boundaries. Clergy who can set appropriate boundaries for themselves are more likely to help church families to set boundaries in turn, to avoid undue pressure on *their* family life.

A teenager worried that his parents did not have enough time off together. The mother said they did not want to leave the youngsters again, having had baby-sitters for parish events. To her it was a double loss, for them as a couple, and for the children.

Parishes could give double messages. One 'talked quite strongly' about taking days off because the previous vicar had become totally swamped. Several parishes, including that one, still arranged regular events on their vicars' day off and constantly asked them to go.

Most families travelled considerable distances to visit their wider families, usually on a day off. No one mentioned a night away. Illness or death of parents had involved more frequent visits or a more prolonged stay usually for the wife. Divorced and remarried grand-parents could mean three or even four sets to visit making them feel, as one wife put it, 'a bit like a juggler'. Her husband added, 'Then sometimes on days off when I don't feel up to it I just look forward to Sunday and getting back to work'.

4. Hobbies and stimulation

The paucity of interests and hobbies was striking. Three spoke of occasional creative gardening like digging a pond. Another found pressures had cut out his daily half-hour garden routine. The garden could have been a relaxation for yet another if he was less stressed, but it was too big to control, which mattered being 'a public house'. He didn't feel he could take an odd hour on a working day, although he was one who spoke of working three sessions on each of six days. Given the choice he would spend time on his day off tinkering with the car. One mentioned amateur dramatics productions but usually connected with the church.

Only one of the men mentioned active sport. A back problem meant he had to give up squash. Three enjoyed walking but this was an occasional, not a regular activity. They were aged between 28 and 47.

Two families mentioned missing the stimulation of friends in or near their previous parish, who would plan outings and include them. After nearly two years one of these families still felt they had no weekly pattern for days off. The other on a large housing estate said that to do anything now they had to initiate it. 'I feel a bit narrow and afraid of becoming a bore with only work and family to talk about.' His wife, mostly confined to their estate with two small children, laughed. 'Think yourself lucky that you have work *and* family. Some of us only have family!' He felt there should be 'more people like us' in their next parish. For most of the others, time with friends seemed confined to holidays.

Two men looked forward to bird watching and painting when the children were a little older. Two were concerned that they found it hard to look forward to anything personal. 'I'd love to have something that's beyond the life of the church.' Outside parish life, their spare time seemed remarkably lonely and lacking in stimulation.

5. Finance

Tight budgets affected what the families could do especially if the wife was not working. One couple said their own entertainment budget was nil. They went out very occasionally.

A wife in the last interview was planning to solve the problem by working on his day off while he looked after their son. Given what all the other families had said about pressure on time together, what would that mean for their relationship and for his 'relaxation'?

6. Reflections on the families' comments

Through experience gained as a work consultant, it was felt that regular supervision could have addressed many of the issues that the couples raised. Boundaries between work and home were a constant conflict both personally for the clergy and between a husband, wife and children. A critical look at their ongoing situation on a consistent basis in supervision could have helped them face and monitor their positions. It could also have helped them to address these with their congregations so that parishioners as well as clergy families were not caught up in an endless round of over-involvement.

However some of the issues would remain as long as clergy had only one day off. Swedish clergy for instance work a five-day week, and the Leadership Group mentioned the need for a shorter working week. Most of our research clergy were working in isolation, from home, in understaffed parishes, and serving a wider public as well as their parishioners. If clients from other professions were bringing these situations to counselling, we would ask what they thought was likely to happen if they continued to work in this way. The lack of both stimulation and contact with friends only increased the pressure.

III. THE REFERENCE GROUPS' COMMENTS ON IDEALISM, INTRUSION AND ISOLATION

In the second round of interviews we looked for the 'pay-offs'. The families shared many positive experiences with us as well as negative ones throughout the interviews. However, they continued to show an underlying cycle of stress-related experiences, powerfully reinforced by other factors.

We summarized the interviews for the Groups under three topics, highlighted in the data, which led to this cycle of stress.

● The idealism of the families and their attempts to be sensitive to other people's expectations, even if it was impracticable to fulfil them: 'It is not their expectations of us, but our expectation of their expectations of us', one wife said.

• The intrusion into family life, which came in many ways.
• The many facets of isolation the families faced.

This cycle was reinforced by a lack of encouragement. Without encouragement clergy would be motivated to go on striving, as they could never know when they were good enough. They also tended to deny their experience of stress as this might not be understood or might be seen as an admission of failure. These issues of motivation and denial will be discussed at a later stage.

1. Idealism

The families' sense of idealism underpinned the whole of their ministry and family life. Their idealism would stem from their faith, wanting to share this with others and to live it out in their daily lives.

Both Reference Groups, however, did not focus on this wider concept of idealism but on the ideal clergy family. This suggests some sort of static model against which a family could be measured without considering the family's context. Walsh[2] showed that any assessment of a family's functioning should be seen as a process linked to the life stage and circumstances of the family, not linked to a set model. She points out , 'There are many paths to healthy family functioning'.

The Pastoral Group suggested that instead of the former paternalistic, autocratic family model, clergy families were moving to a more shared family responsibility, even though this was very hard to put into practice. The Group also discussed ways in which the clergy family became the model for the Church.

The issue of expectations showed a gender divide in the Group. The women turned this issue back onto the families saying that they had to recognize their expectations of others' expectations. Clergy family life, 'like bereavement', could only be worked through by the family itself. The Group said that once wives understood the central issue of 'what God expects of me' and that role as self is accepted,

---

2 Walsh, F. (1993) 'Conceptualisation of normal family processes', in *Normal Family Processes* (2nd edn pp. 3–69). London: Guilford Press.

everything else would fall into place and lead to greater spiritual health.

This response suggested a level of maturity in clergy wives that could take years to achieve as this distinction of role, according to the data, was anything but clear-cut. Church members or the public could see them in their public role at any time. They never knew when. They might feel they had begun to understand that 'role', but still flounder. The families' discussions suggested they were constantly struggling to find a balance between their own family life and chosen schedule, and unexpected demands and intrusions. Even those with considerable experience in secular jobs, used to juggling situations on a daily basis, found this balance particularly difficult. The reality of such experiences was shown in the study of local elected councillors' families explored in Chapter 4.

The men in the Pastoral Group, however, thought that people did not look to the family for a model 'as much as we think'. They felt that it is a turning point for the families when they realize the expectations are there but so are 'our expectations of their expectations'. They considered expectations came more from non-congregational members of the parish, but the data suggested these came primarily from members of the congregation. Neither Group discussed the dilemma that families had in assessing an appropriate response to expectations of whatever sort, itself a stressful process. One Leadership Group member acknowledged that it is the invidious pressures that are far more difficult to handle.

The Leadership Group, having suggested that many clergy are controlling of families, asked if the ideal clergy family meant partners sharing the clergy job or sharing in the life of the church. Is it a vocation for both of them? They spoke of the ideal model of shared ordained ministry. Although this all gave the sense of a static model, one member said a bishop's family could be a model, giving permission to clergy families to be themselves, and so liberating them.

The Leadership Group raised various ideas and questions. If the family were not involved in the church, they thought this could affect the priest's job. In contrast, the wife could be a rebel and be admired. They wondered if it is stress or rivalry when the wife is more capable and able to make decisions than the priest. Is the ideal family linked to class structure, as clergy now come from a different background – suggesting a static model? Families might be 'ideal' clergy families when young but are certainly not now.

If this final statement is valid, it raises the question, 'what has brought about the change?' Would it help to maintain their idealism if the families had a secure base? The comment on different backgrounds was not unpacked but a possible perspective is given below.[3] Our research families came from a variety of backgrounds. The Group had asked if we were lucky that all the families were so committed and what refusal rate we had had. In fact all families contacted had been willing to take part but some did not meet our criteria if, for example, older children had left home and were not available for interviews.

2. Intrusion

In the Pastoral Group the women said intrusion into the family was extremely real, but there were strategies to deal with it. Otherwise it led to a protective insulation against criticism. The sense of victimization could then become a barrier to asking for available help. The men in the Group thought the families should educate parishioners that the house was a home and not just there for everyone to use. There might also be intrusion into the couple's relationship, as well as into the home, if people tried to 'get at' the priest through his wife. For clergy children such attacks and criticism could leave them very upset and helpless as their comments show.

The Leadership Group saw insulation not as the safeguard in the unusual situation of a clergy family, as the Pastoral Group suggested, but as the warmth and protection that is a normal concept for any home. They asked if a clergy home is as insulated as our summary indicated, as wives are working and the home may have voluntary/ paid help. They asked, 'How do you break the cycle of stress?' Does the family close in and put on a good face until it becomes severe? A final comment, noted on the flip chart without its overall context, said 'what husbands and wives are for – to bash each other'.

---

3   University of Cambridge Alumni Magazine (Michaelmas Term 2004) No. 43 *Profile Portrait in oil*. The chief executive of BP, John Browne's comment to an American audience may throw light on the Leadership Group's statement: 'Perhaps being British and because we employ so many graduates of Cambridge and Oxford means we tend not to wear our hearts on our sleeves. We don't express much emotion'. Crockford's Clerical Directory shows that many older or retired clergy were Oxbridge graduates.

3. Isolation

The men in the Pastoral Group asked if isolation was self-inflicted and said there was need for supervision and support groups. The women said help was there but not sought. They felt the pay-offs would be revitalizing and needed to be developed: the good marriages and good family life we had described, with members concerned for one another and interested in each other's development and achievements, including progress in the parish.

The Leadership Group took the question of support very seriously. They considered that cries for help must be followed up. There also needed to be a day-to-day safety net and a system of review before that stage was reached, as a means of relating to clergy and families on a regular basis. These safeguards were particularly important for families in difficult parishes. They emphasized the importance of taking time off. They suggested that teams could provide mutual support through joint meetings with partners to counteract isolation. They asked how the leadership related to clergy families and one member raised the question of whether committee work meant that the leadership avoided pastoral work. This avoidance could be due to other demands on their time or could indicate a more direct avoidance given the many uncertainties they expressed. The idea that the leadership should be directly involved with clergy families in this way would probably be impractical in any case. The research clergy were asking for professional supervision and support from the leadership. Separate support systems would be appropriate for the families. The crucial point from the Leadership Group's response was that no immediate suggestions were made about how these support systems might be put in place, or who should be directly responsible for ensuring that they were established.

In their first meeting the Leadership Group had said that there would be value in saying how the families operate as a family. Despite the cycle of stress, our research families were functioning well in terms of the main criteria of healthy family functioning: e.g. appropriate family boundaries, support to one another, good communication and encouragement. The question then remains, how is the church as an organization helping clergy families to maintain healthy functioning? If it is not doing so, and underlying support systems are so tentative and vary between dioceses, a further question is how do clergy families survive in such an uncertain context?

16 Conflict and Health

I. CONFLICT

1. The job comes first

The families emphasized the importance of ensuring a day off each week. They felt that interrupted or missed days off were 'the nature of a lot of problems we have in the family'. The pace of life, the constant pressure and unclear boundaries were underlying sources of family conflict. One man spelt out the dilemma the families faced. 'We need time to maintain a sensible balance to family life. In the past few months several clergy friends and contemporaries have gone through traumatic marriage breakdowns. There is a huge strain because the previous pattern was church first and family second. I have said clearly that my vocation, as a husband and a father are first priorities. The vocation to the church is number two.' Another wife, herself a clergy daughter, said that for her parents the church came first, and it still did for her older sister as a clergy wife.

The teenage children in one family spoke graphically about how they had to learn to surrender both their own time and their Dad. 'We've had to put up with disappointment, cutting holidays short, leaving late or being split up as a family because Dad can't do something.' 'We had a day at the Test Match planned this summer. A really big day for me! I'd been looking forward to it for ages. But he had the funeral of a personal contact and it would have looked bad if he hadn't done it. People would think he cared more about his family than his job. I believe he does but he has to keep a very fine balance between the two and ends up doing a lot more for the parish. Trying to tell 200 people the family's sitting at home and not very happy is harder than actually saying to us, "I'm sorry but I've got to do it now". We just learn to take it.'

His mother said that several years before things 'family-wise had been pretty horrendous'. They had terrible tensions and anxieties over the balance of time and the ability to talk it out. 'Even when the tension was past you'd feel such a heap and be so mad and resentful that you wouldn't even enjoy the good bits. At times he would have pulled out of ministry because we were actually more important than the job. Although from the things the children have said today it appears we do come second, I know that fundamentally we don't'. Her husband agreed. 'I said I would leave rather than ruin our home. Since then we've tried to cobble together a better working arrangement and find ways of living with all the different pressures on us'. Her perpetual nagging that he ought to spend more time with the children was once seen as a 'singularly powerful factor in the problem'. From his point of view if he'd left because the family was suffering too much 'it would have been an easy option for me to pass the responsibility for pulling out over to her. I felt she would have had to carry a lot of that burden and guilt. At different stages now the balance is still wrong but the acceptance is better and the resentment is less.'

As already mentioned, the need for anonymity has dictated that the story should be told under topics rather than the whole picture for each family. It is not easy therefore within confidentiality guidelines to show specifically how difficult it had been for each of these families to fulfil the intention of putting the family first. However, in the last interview it was the father just mentioned who was 'appalled to see', from his comments on the flip chart, that the year had held nothing personal for him. Work had dominated everything. The job had come first and they were still fighting to find time together as a family. They had 'cobbled together a better working arrangement' and 'found ways of living with all the different pressures on us'. The conflict had diminished, but the children's perception about coming second, intentionally or not, may have been the actual picture. Within two or three years the two eldest children would probably have left home. They had accommodated to the situation; he had not left the ministry.

2. The children's involvement and the distance regulator

Dr John Byng Hall[1] speaks about how children can be drawn into their parents' relationship in a go-between role and become a

---

1 Byng-Hall, J. (1980) *Symptom Bearer as Marital Distance Regulator: Clinical Implications.* Family Process, 19, 355–365.

'distance regulator'. This idea appeared in another family's comments. They described a complex pattern of support, conflict and cross-generational involvement. A wife felt she could help her husband put the brakes on when his ideas ran away with him. When members came with church issues it could be hard to unravel these from their personal problems and perceptions, and from their attitude to authority or to her husband. Then he needed help. She could stand back and say, 'Enough is enough; you've bent my ear on this three times, no more'. The difficulty was distinguishing between helping him, and telling him how to do his job which he found very hard to take from anyone unless he had asked for their advice.

This distinction was especially blurred when she was in 'bulldozer mode', having come home from work tired, negative and bad-tempered. He and their ten-year-old son would 'have a session' together which he saw as the two of them helping each other to cope, rather than helping his wife. She also found support from their son. 'We can have a very adult conversation and he's a helpful person to talk things out with.'

The dilemma for this couple was not only the appropriate closeness or distance in their personal relationship but also in the unofficial professional relationship they had developed because the husband had no other regular professional support. He had worked alone for 11 years until just before the last interview. When her advice or involvement in his work became entangled with their personal relationship, the son was drawn in by both of them.

The husband acknowledged that other factors influenced his wife's mood linked to life stages in the family and his job. She had just returned to her previous job after having her children and parts of this were quite stressful. They were also unsettled, feeling it was time to move.

The accumulated pressures of living for ten years in the inner city with 'a home that in principle is always open' had also made her say recently that she did not like living in a vicarage. That had hurt him. He felt she had known from the start that she would be marrying a clergyman and, again in principle, 'known what she was letting herself in for, not like people becoming vicars after years of marriage. Situations change and you find out more about it, but I would find it very hard if she turned out to be allergic to vicarages.'

This family's experience highlights several issues that could be emphasized by those responsible for clergy training and supervision.

Supervision could have provided a more appropriate 'distance regulator' for this couple because it would have freed the wife from her sense of responsibility to provide professional support. It would also have freed his son to be a ten-year-old. The strict code of confidentiality in supervision would also allow the husband to explore his wife's concerns about the pressures of vicarage life and find possible new boundaries to protect their home in view of her new work commitment.

Their children, like many of the research children of all ages, were highly involved in the church and in supporting the priest's ministry in various ways. The research shows how important the children's role could be at times in a priest's work. The children themselves were aware that, for them, everything depended on the clergy ministry being successfully maintained otherwise they might have to move house again or, worse still, not have a home. Appropriate professional boundaries for clergy might reduce tension and make it less necessary for them to be drawn in. If supervisors were alerted to the children's involvement, this is an area they could explore with clergy in the future.

3. Emotional support, active silence and whose responsibility?

A different pattern was shown in another couple's relationship. They had a two-year-old, she was pregnant, and her husband was one of those who spoke of working morning, noon, and night. He would know she was feeling stressed because she was 'a bit grumpy', or more demanding and emotional, and he saw this as a silent accusation. His sense of guilt led him to respond defensively, making it harder for him to support her.

They had just begun to recognize this pattern and change their reactions. He was trying to keep an hour each afternoon as family time, but later said that it was almost always 'eaten up' by work. He would tell her sometimes that other people were under more stress as many commuting fathers in their area were away all day. He had fallen into the trap of focussing on one aspect of their situation and making comparisons, rather than taking an overall view. He knew this wasn't helpful and was trying to listen to her instead.

'I feel it'll just sound like hypocrisy if I say anything because I might not be able to live up to my promises. But afterwards I do something really helpful like cleaning the house or buying her flowers.' He realized that his silence might make his wife think he was not interested and not listening.

She said it was good to have practical help and she realized that he did things to show that he was concerned but she did not know until later that he *was* going to do them. As a result she felt that if she was 'down' the only answer was to sort it out by herself. Sometimes she felt resentful that she could not get through to him without 'the dynamic coming into play that he hears it as an accusation. Even though I'm saying that there isn't an accusation, maybe there is. I don't know. I still can't get the *emotional* support and find it hard to live without it, especially at the moment'.

The pattern of men finding it easier to offer practical rather than emotional support may link to Pollack and Gilligan's[2] finding that men find threat in closeness whereas women find threat in isolation. The Double ABCX Model of stress, outlined in Chapter 5, looks at emotional, esteem and network support as resources for the family. For clergy wives their network support is often diffuse, especially after a move. This of course could be the same for any family in any new situation but they would not also have the public role and the pressure on the home.

Almost all our research families lived at a distance from extended family and any immediate emotional support they might give. They were expected to give emotional support to a wide variety of people, known and unknown, so support for one another was particularly important, but paradoxically this could put an additional pressure on their relationship.

This couple saw that his stress began with his work schedule, which then contributed to her stress. She was left with the underlying responsibility for 'just about everything else that happens in the home including finance, our social life, family birthdays and visits to family and friends'. Her husband said he did take 'some of the responsibility'. Their discussion echoed Patricia Hewitt's[3] comments that 'the key question is not who does the domestic work but who is *responsible* for the second shift in the home, the unpaid hours for working couples'.

2   Pollak, S. and Gilligan, C. (1982) 'Images of Violence in Thematic Apperception Test Stories' *Journal of Personality and Social Psychology,* 742, 159–167.
3   Hewitt, P. (1993) *About Time: The Revolution in Work and Family Life.* London: Institute for Public Policy Research Rivers Oram Press.

She quotes from widespread research suggesting that, for four out of five couples, the female partner still takes overall responsibility. Two issues were significant. This couple had *not* conformed to gender stereotypes before their children were born when the wife also had a very demanding job. Responsibility had been shared. The husband's final comment was that perhaps they needed to sort this out, but then that he thought it might actually be conscious on his part. In church, despite delegation, 'in the end if anything goes wrong I have to carry the can and pick up the pieces. At home I don't want that responsibility, I want somewhere where I can just kind of be one of the workers, where someone else does the organizing'.

The Pastoral Group emphasized how important it was for clergy couples to be honest with one another. This couple were attempting, often with considerable hurt and uncertainty, to understand one another, and be honest about their own part in the process. Despite their efforts the job still came first. The husband was unable to share family responsibilities and was seldom there to be 'just one of the workers'.

For this couple the husband may need to thrash out the situation in work consultancy or supervision so that he ensures more time for the family. He may also need to consider how he can provide space for his wife to be just 'one of the workers, where someone else does the organizing', especially with the pressure on their home from his job. It could be particularly difficult for them to set appropriate boundaries while handling a series of life cycle changes: their recent move, a new job for him in an ecumenical church, and a new baby arriving. Equally, it could be a good moment for them to be clear with the new congregation about the importance of family time. Again this gives a message to parishioners about setting priorities that protect family life.

If the pressures of the job and the absence of boundaries affected the priest's attitudes and behaviour adversely in a situation of this sort, this would be a further subtle and telling way in which intrusion came into the home.

It is interesting to note that this may be one of the differences for couples where the wife is the priest. What would happen to the marriage and the family then if family time was always 'eaten into'? Is there more understanding from the laity if she says she must set time aside for the family? Would the husband need to take over responsibility for all the organizational issues? What would happen if both partners were ordained?

4. Organizational and family life cycles – Management who put People first

Their story also raises issues of the interface of family and organizational life cycles. The increasing rate of clergy marriage breakdown has been a particular concern of the Church's leadership, and was one factor prompting our research. Organizational literature questions whether or not employees, at key life cycle stages, should be expected to take on high demands or lose promotion prospects. This has mainly applied to women's careers but, writing about dual-earner couples, Lewis[4] suggested that 'corporations need to appraise the life cycles of all employees just as they do the cycles of product lines, and revise corporate career paths in relation to those differing phases'.

The church may also need to consider seriously the effect of high demands on clergy at these key stages when their partners are also expected to have a public role and face at least a degree of intrusion into the home. The discussion above took place less than a year after a move to the husband's first living, with the added complexities of ecumenical sharing, a house on the church complex, and the imminent birth of their second child. They were both aware of the problem and were attempting to address it. If they had not felt able to do this, or had not realized what was causing the tension between them, their future relationship could well be threatened.

A fundamental issue is whether the church, or any organization, should also take some responsibility for its demands. In the journal *Human Resources* in 1995,[5] Professor Charles Handy asks if, in the future, work at the core of organizations will leave so little time for personal life that 'management may become a celibate career. I don't mean no relationships, but it could mean no conflicting commitments . . . I don't think organizations will be able to demand that degree of dedication for more than ten years'. The subtitle of the *Human Resources* journal is *For Management who put People first*.

In Chapter 4 we saw how these issues were viewed in other contexts. We noted Jolly's[6] question of whether family men were

---

4 Lewis, S., Izraeli, N. and Hootsmans, H. (eds) (1992) *Dual Earner Families*. London: Sage.

5 Handy, C. (November/December 1995) in *Human Resources*. London: Martin Leach Publishing..

6 Jolly, R. (19987) *Military Man, Family Man: Crown Property?* London: Brassey's Defence Publishers.

wanted in the Military because of the pressures involved and conflict with family life. Kirk and Leary, like Horsman, commented on a clergyman being married to his wife *and* the church, models of the ideal domestic relationship but totally available for people's needs. The American Cornerstone Project suggested that there was no 'theology of the married priesthood'. The question is, 'Does the Church want to convey an image of family life in which one partner is primarily married to the job?'

5.   The work must be done and what price success

Two teenagers spoke of how their father's job influenced family conflict. Their father had spoken of 'horrendous rows' particularly between his wife and teenage daughter. He felt the pace of life was too high, they were all trying to cram too much in and they did not 'take time to do what we are doing now, to sit down together as a family, relax and understand where each other is' – an interesting perspective on the research interviews. He felt he and his wife thought quite carefully about how they were going to deal with particular situations or crises, and tried to let just one parent deal with a situation so the other could remain calm. If he was at home he was often in his study while his wife and daughter were talking and would only come out if the shouting got too loud. If he had someone in his study and there were arguments, his wife found it very difficult. The daughter's perspective was that if he had to come out and intervene then 'the thing he is most worried about is getting his work done'.

One son said that they hardly ever went out as a family because they always argued. He thought this was just how they were as a family rather than because they were a clergy family. Then he added, 'Maybe it's 'cos of Dad's job. He always gets angry because there aren't many people coming to church and stuff. Then he gets a bit cross and takes it out on us usually'. Another example of stress passed on to children. His mother thought the children were the main source of conflict between her and her husband. She mostly only shouted at him about the children. When both children were there, there was more friction and a lot of 'nit-picking' and intolerance. They all contributed. They hadn't any time at weekends because her husband was always in work mode. It would be nice if they had a whole weekend and he could relax at home.

In other families, conflict, sibling rivalry and 'picking on each other' were mentioned but not always specifically linked to being clergy families. One father was aware that his daughter was growing up and perhaps she needed to argue. In his job he saw confrontational situations in other's lives and was 'able to advise myself very nicely after I've been through it. I just wish I could put theory and practice together in dealing with confrontation at home, and back off a bit and let her have her say and be herself'. He too spoke of the pressure of the job affecting their family life.

6. Reflections

The themes recur: constant work, the job coming first, lack of boundaries, life lived in public, isolation, conflict in the family. Isolation could happen in the midst of general friendship from the parish. If couples felt it was difficult to have close friends in the parish, the sense of isolation would be still more intense. In three families mentioned above it was the *wife's* reaction that was seen as the focus of the problem, even though each family spoke of how significantly the job contributed to her stress. In consultation, other patterns of support and responsibility could be explored, rather than 'her stress makes her grumpy' or 'in bulldozer mode'. The families' comments related to specific issues but should be seen as part of the whole picture.

The hidden issues of conflict were highlighted in an article in the *Church Times* on 7 June 1996 quoting from a report in the *Anglican Journal* in Canada. The story of marital difficulties experienced by Canon Michael Green and his wife in the 1980s had been mentioned during a course she was conducting there. These difficulties had resulted at one stage in a broken tooth for him and a black eye for her. 'Rosemary at that time had a temper. I would not initiate (violence) but I would respond to it', Canon Green is quoted as saying. 'I shouldn't have done it.' They had been working energetically in different spheres, and 'not being very good at communicating with each other. I take my full share of responsibility for that'. The article said that both knew a divorce would end Canon Green's credibility as an evangelist and their marriage was 'now gloriously sorted out'. Mrs Green subsequently became a Christian counsellor.

A letter in reply to the article the following week came from a student member of their church in Oxford at the time. 'My wife and I (now both ordained priests) and many others were aware of the incredible workload they undertook – reckoned by a colleague to be about 96 hours a week including running a church, student missions and his prolific writing, as well as his ministry to many who came to them for help.

'Many saw their marriage difficulties as a nearly inevitable consequence of their rare gifts of service; thousands are still in their debt.'

The Greens were honest and courageous enough in due time to share their experience. They and the couple in I.3 above had worked on their difficulties, but a number of incidents described in this whole section suggest that conflict and even violence may be more widespread than they appear. The incidents also suggest that one possible source of each partner's anger may be the open-ended nature of the job. It is interesting that in the letter above the writer speaks of the incredible workload *they* undertook ... as well as *his* ministry to many who came to *them* for help.

Theological colleges may need to address directly with couples how their perceptions and reactions to 'what they are letting themselves in for' may change over time especially if wives are in their early 20s when they marry. The family trees showed that the husbands had married in their mid-20s or later. Discussion at the training stage about monitoring ongoing change could give couples permission to check out regularly with one another how the job was affecting their home and relationship. This is particularly important for couples if they 'did not see people outside the parish regularly enough for others to know their situation'.

If stress arises from the priest's job, and consultants are acknowledging the stress, they are providing a more secure base for the couple simply through the acknowledgement. Discussing these issues when the pressure is low rather than when it is high is likely to be much more effective.

II. THE REFERENCE GROUPS' RESPONSE ON MOTIVATION AND DENIAL, AND REFLECTIONS

We were looking at the whole system of the Church to explain the power of the cycle of stress for clergy families, and the emotional and physical distress that follows, and we emphasized this approach to the

Reference Groups. The intensity of this cycle led the Pastoral Group to question if we had fed information to the families. We explained again the openness of the questions.

The issues of motivation and denial were highlighted in the second part of our summary to the Groups. What made the clergy work at such an unremitting pace?

We had developed two hypotheses. First, if priests never knew when they were doing enough because of lack of encouragement or affirmation, this could constantly motivate such idealistic people to work harder. Second, the absence of a forum for discussing stresses, difficulties or seeming failures might mean clergy families denied these issues, fearing parishioners or the hierarchy could be dismissive about them. The issues might also be too painful or complicated to address except in the receptive setting of confidential supervision.

1. Motivation

The whole Pastoral Group was very surprised that, with two or three notable exceptions, there was no encouragement. The men in particular agreed that there was a danger of clergy becoming workaholics, and all the Group said clear boundaries, supervision, and support groups could alleviate some of the pressures. As there was no obvious end product, they saw a need for setting aims and objectives, as well as having feedback and encouragement from the hierarchy to provide ongoing motivation.

They suggested framing the pattern of motivation differently. They said that if there is no feedback to clergy:

1. Idealism would be the catalyst. If there is also
2. Lack of encouragement, and
3. Lack of effective supervision, this is likely to lead to clergy 'working beyond their limits'.

If, on the other hand, the lack of encouragement led to idealism ceasing, there might be a complete 'slacking off', possibly resulting in the problems of various kinds already mentioned.

They asked if this was a point in history where there was a particular generational divide, as younger and older clergy were seen to be working to two contrasting models of ministry that might provide or prevent motivation:

- The ascetic ideal where 24 hours belong to God. In training this might be portrayed as boundary-less. There was also an implication of the priest as his own master with no interference from the hierarchy.

- The younger generation reflecting a 'professional, boundaried, supervised model', with everything 'weighted, costed, timed and planned', and clergy and laity co-constructing the Church's needs together. This would ultimately de-motivate as it 'was missing out on holiness'.

The Pastoral Group pointed out that 24 hours can be dedicated to God but that includes nurturing oneself and one's family.

The Leadership Group said these models of ministry were recognizable. Newly-trained ordinands now worked to a business model, which was unspiritual, and older ordinands have experience of job appraisal from their secular employment.

2. Denial

In our summary, permission to admit situations and not to deny them had referred to stresses, difficulties and perceived failure. It was not possible for the families to address these if the system itself ignored them, or disbelieved them and dismissed their seriousness. Both Groups, however, linked the issue of denial to permission to admit personal failure, disappointment and weakness. This turned the issue back onto the families, giving the issue a quite different meaning.

The importance of different levels of the organization considering its own response to clergy family stress was only touched on briefly. The Leadership Group said there was a need to monitor situations especially in tough parishes. The Pastoral Group mentioned the need for a day-to-day provision for support. This would be helped by a mutuality of care between clergy families and congregations, as well as support groups, but need not necessarily involve the hierarchy. They suggested isolation could be self-inflicted.

However, this would only be so if clear systems and ongoing communication were available, but ignored by the families. The section on a Secure Base showed that if people are heard and given respectful support, rather than being blamed or seen as inept or failing, then those in any field of life would feel more confident to act on their own initiative. They would also be much less likely to seek help.

3. The pay-offs

Throughout the second round of interviews the families emphasized the many facets of the 'pay-offs'. In particular, they highlighted the caring and supportive aspects of their family lives, and their sense of growing competence in ministry, especially when there were positive responses in parish life. They valued, too, the very natural opportunities their position gave them to talk to other people about faith and the privilege of being 'set aside' to give them more time to do this.

The Pastoral Group felt that the sense of purpose, direction, belonging and the conviction that God is in control gave a meaning to life, which helped clergy and their wives get through stress. They felt the families only speaking of positives gave a false impression. Equally the pay-offs needed to be developed. The Group added to the pay-offs that children learnt to mix with a great range of people. They were also introduced much earlier than usual to the 'shadow side of life', from which other children might be protected, and had the opportunity to learn that people could come through difficult times.

4. The generational divide

The Pastoral Group had suggested that the different models of ministry and other tensions might stem from a generational divide. This seemed to raise a fundamental issue, which we shall touch on briefly. The Pastoral Group suggested that the older generation of clergy are working within an ascetic model with the clergyman as expert, whereas the younger generation are following more of a business model and working in partnership with laity. This suggestion of a changed model of ministry may reflect a 'shift' of paradigm or framework for clergy, and could be at the heart of a generational divide.

In *Grappling THE Gap*, Margaret Mead[7] put forward a hypothesis which may help to explain this paradigm shift. She suggested that for those born before World War II, space travel, nuclear weapons and an age of computers had been new discoveries. For those born since 1946 these were not new. The younger generation had never known

7 Mead, M. (1972) *Grappling the Gap*, Paper given to American Field Service scholarship students at their New York conference.

anything else. This was a condition that for the first time in history existed throughout the world. As a consequence the child would not become the man his father was. 'Even if the child were to pursue the same occupation, he would live in a different way . . . he would see the world differently. This is THE generation gap'. She points out that although tremendous changes have taken place in the past, this has never been on a global scale 'and will probably never happen again'.

The majority of those with leadership and management roles in the Anglican Church were born during or possibly before World War II (Crockford's *Clerical Directory*). The clergy couples of the research families were all born after Mead's dividing line of 1946. The data in no way suggest that the research clergy were 'missing out on holiness' but rather that they were searching for a new paradigm or framework for ministry.

An interesting link between the Generation Gap, working all hours and days off, is given in a sermon in 2005 by the former archdeacon of York, George Austin.[8] He says, 'For many of us, trained and ordained in a different age, the work of the priesthood was the priority – even on a day off if the need arose. The idea of dividing each working day into three, morning, afternoon and evening, and working on only two of the three, would have been incomprehensible. A bishop once said to me, "Oh, I never take a day off." "And which of the other nine commandments can we break?" I asked him with some interest and anticipation. He didn't enlighten me.'

Another aspect of the generational divide may be that clergy, like most young professionals, tend to be more involved with their families than older clergy ever expected to be.

III. HEALTH

1. Pressure and privacy

The families spoke of a wide variety of health problems, although no specific question on health was asked. One vicar experienced a 'nervous breakdown' between the second and third interviews. Another had six weeks off with stress some time before the research. He had more than quadrupled his congregation but was concerned

---

8   Austin, G. (2005) Sermon preached on 17 May to the Retired Clergy Association.

that 'the charismatic services would have gone off the rails unless I set limits and held everything together. I felt a terrific pressure.'

Both these vicars said it was difficult not to have privacy at home when they were ill. 'If you commuted to work you would come home to get better but if you have a place where you work and live ... certainly I sometimes crossed the road to avoid people asking how I was. It was hard for them to understand.'

2. The long-term picture

When we asked about future concerns, most families spoke of the impact on their health of living long term with the constant demands of the job. This was an over-riding concern even though most of the priests were in their 30s or early 40s. One said, 'Seeing what happens to many men in their 40s and 50s, the anxiety is there of will I make it through this stage?' Three couples felt vulnerable after the death of a contemporary. A wife commented, 'With all the pressures you wonder how you'd stay afloat if health became a factor.' Another mentioned 'the delicate balance we live on'. There had been no tragedies, large or small, in her wider family. 'It just might happen, and life that feels really good now could all be thrown into chaos.'

Even minor illnesses could have a debilitating effect. A priest had problems with allergies for five months. A drains problem had made the house increasingly damp, especially the study – the second instance of attention to damp being delayed. The allergies were 'getting him down'. In his previous parish he had not slept properly for 18 months and this was happening again. 'The only way I can cope (in an isolated situation in the inner city) is by working morning, afternoon and night. It's a vicious circle because then my performance drops and I get bad-tempered'.

A husband developed a back problem and had to give up squash. 'Nothing else is as fulfilling', and he felt less fit. His wife was younger and concerned that her backache could become more severe. Several instances of significant back problems were mentioned.

3. When the pressure is off

Symptoms emerged once the pressure was temporarily removed. 'I felt I was working too hard and spent our holiday last week having headaches and heartburn, letting stress out because I stopped and flopped.' Another found his suspected ulcer was clear. 'All stress related – ulcers are. I had the symptoms when I was relaxing. It was an increasing worry for nine months. The doctor said my irritable bowel syndrome was probably through stress.' Later he had a wisdom tooth extracted 'I was fine straight afterwards, did too much and then suffered for it.' It is interesting to link this to an original aim of St Luke's Hospital for the Clergy, which was to treat them quickly and get them back to work *as soon as possible.*

After a demanding week running a holiday club, one man had chest pains and discovered he had high blood pressure. His doctor said both conditions would be aggravated by the stress of the job and his workload. He was the one incumbent who had a specific, additional job which had been 'set up in haste' by the bishop and grown 'beyond all intention'. The bishop, however, said it could not be full-time. It made his wife feel they should move.

4.   The pressure of understanding the task

Both Reference Groups spent considerable time talking about how clergy understood their task. One vicar spoke of the stress of his first years in a parish and 'finding out what we were supposed to be doing. I found it incredibly hard. My neck was permanently tight and I spent hours in outpatients having physiotherapy.' His wife had post-natal depression at the time. Who gave them guidance on his job? 'Nobody really! I had to find my own way. The bloke before me had done such a good job and I felt I was messing it up'. He was obviously seen as a capable person by the hierarchy as he was offered a job with significant responsibility for his next appointment.

5.   Children's illness

Several of the children had serious illnesses. The daughter who was seriously ill in hospital just before her father's induction has been mentioned. Another was in hospital with pneumonia, at first thought to be meningitis. A third was on 'massive doses of steroids' for asthma. Her mother said, 'She had a certain lack of confidence due to the illness and found it hard adjusting to her new school'. At an official function the bishop's wife had said, 'You must be very worried about her'. It was 'a very obvious thing to say but nobody else had said it. I hadn't acknowledged the worry myself so her acknowledgement was helpful'. The acknowledgement of difficulties by those in authority is a key factor in overcoming the Accommodation Syndrome.

A son had hay fever and a problem with bed-wetting. Clinic checks made no difference. Had he been disturbed by the frequent coming and going to the vicarage each evening as well as being singled out for criticism by the congregation for doing things done by most children in his age group? Another child had 'nothing major' but was described as always being in the wars. A nine-year-old child fell and damaged her ankle, which took a long time to heal.

6.   Wives' illness and the public role, pregnancy and isolation

The wives mentioned several illnesses: one developed asthma, ongoing eye treatment following haemorrhaging affected a second wife, a third had hay fever.

For another couple the personal and the public aspect of the job became entwined over health issues. The wife in her early 30s had surgery for a collapsed lung. This 'turned my husband's life upside down. Rumours went round that I had cancer. Some people were very aggressive, as though somehow we were to blame, which was an additional pressure. I don't fully understand that yet'. A churchwarden got most worked up that nothing had been said in services. 'We thought most people knew. In one of the other churches the churchwarden said, "Our thoughts and prayers are with you", after reading the lesson, which was very nice. Some people were hurt that they weren't asked to do something, but non-specific offers of help are difficult to cope with.'

His wife felt a lot of people in the parishes were very concerned about her illness. Even though this couple were in their 30s with small children, a fellow clergyman suggested to them that people see clergy as parental figures and if anything happens it shatters their illusions.

Her husband commented on another issue. 'When people asked how we were I had to assess very quickly whether they wanted to know or whether there was something they wanted to say that was more important. That's by the nature of being a clergyman rather than a banker or something. People expect me, understandably so, to be reasonably available when they want me to talk about their particular needs. Another pressure.'

The most striking issue, however, was the number of problems the families faced around pregnancy. 'I took months and months to recover from the birth and was in a lot of pain. I just assumed that was what happened.' Her husband painted the wider picture. 'We didn't live close to the church so she didn't bump into people. We'd only been there about five months, not long enough to make good friends. It was a very difficult time.' His wife became apprehensive about her second baby.

Another wife was ill for five months during her second pregnancy with a serious threat of miscarriage. Both parents had gastric flu during that time and the baby didn't grow for two weeks. 'People in the congregation were superb but we couldn't always take up offers to look after our little girl, as it takes time for her to build up relationships. The archdeacon and his wife gave support but churchwardens did nothing at all.' The two-year-old was always ill and had never slept, and her mother was anxious about the new baby's birth. This baby had very bad asthma and croup, which was very worrying, and had tests for cystic fibrosis.

Then shortly after her birth the husband's serious back problem recurred. 'If I hadn't been a clergyman it would have been much easier to stop and lie down when the problem first arose. But my curate moved as the baby was born. I couldn't give up on everything. It was worse by the time I did.' Once his new curate came he felt 'freedom to be ill. I was on my back for ten days, in a lot of pain for ten weeks and in physiotherapy for five months. I couldn't lift the children. Some people clearly linked it to the lack of support I felt in the parish'. He also had asthma before their holiday. Life stages coincided: the curate left and the baby arrived, but church demands had taken priority.

In the late stage of pregnancy with her third baby, one wife suffered back problems needing hospital visits three times a week for nearly two years. They had help from churchwardens with transport and cleaning but few other offers of practical help. The husband said his wife also 'went to see a long-term clergyman friend of ours at least once a month, which has given her support outside the parish and her immediate circle of friends in a relaxed way.' At least two other wives had counselling during some part of the research interviews, and two mentioned post-natal depression.

The isolation of many of the couples seemed highly significant during pregnancy difficulties. The doctor had been 'very off-hand' after a wife had an early miscarriage. 'You don't have friends around so his attitude is important.' There was extra pressure the following year because of the miscarriage as she was ill during a subsequent pregnancy. They had 'no proper holiday because of the baby arriving'.

The experience of those two years, in a demanding, isolated situation, meant the lack of holiday had added significance.

Another mother had had a threatened miscarriage in her second pregnancy so the baby had become very precious. The child was involved in an accident several years later, and the experience 'all came back', seeing her little girl in pain. She had mentioned waiting five years to become pregnant, reflecting an issue clergy wives have mentioned over many years. Two sets of parents in the research had adopted one or more children although they did not specifically link this to difficulty in conceiving.

7.   Reflections on the families' comments on health

We had made every effort to recruit families who were not receiving help for current problems, but nine of our 20 families showed a serious physical or emotional symptom of stress for one or more members. All the other families, without exception, gave indications of excessive strain. This corresponded with the American research projects mentioned in Chapter 4 section III.

Three couples mentioned the bishop or archdeacon knowing of their problem and expressing support, yet the general isolation continued. When couples felt so isolated, the supportive comments of a bishop's wife or dismissive comments from a GP had added importance. Support from congregations could be excellent, but the couples were constantly aware of people's hidden agendas, and the difficulty of saying very much about themselves. Their loss of privacy during more serious illness was a particular factor in recovery. Several couples experienced moves immediately before or after the birth of a child.

The lack of exercise for priests, aged 30 to mid-40s, because of time constraints generally and at weekends may have a long-term effect on health. Only one wife mentioned taking regular exercise.

Parents seldom seemed to find time to consider the significance of events: 'something I hadn't actually acknowledged for myself'; 'I wasn't eating, darling? That's interesting'; and, 'You don't think about the year until you have to think about it'.

The health concerns highlighted in the data add weight to the need for professional consultation so that clergy are able to monitor their work rather than 'all the stress coming out on holiday'. The issues may help Church leaders at each level to look carefully at the implications of many of these experiences, and consider ways in which additional help could be given to support the families.

17 The Third Interviews

I. THE THIRD INTERVIEWS

At the end of the second round of interviews it seemed that clergy families were largely left to draw on their own spiritual, emotional and practical resources for support in most areas of their ministry and family life. The interviews suggested that their isolation and idealism might make clergy and their families cover up any problems that emerged, aware of the strong pressure to be exemplary. The extent of their difficulties was therefore hard to judge.

However, the conveners of supervision groups for clergy counsellors, covering several dioceses, had emphasized to us the very serious nature of problems the counsellors were encountering. In the third interviews the Pastoral Group expanded on inappropriate sexual behaviour, mentioning cases of flashing, wife-swapping and abuse. The Leadership Group had talked of significant debt and clergy marriage breakdown, and one member spoke of the devastating impact it would have on the Church if the severity of the issues were known.

A Leadership Group member said that the leadership were giving responsibility for these serious issues to counsellors 'who are carrying the burden on our behalf'. One of the Group then asked, 'Who is solving the problems?' As we have seen, confidentiality means those serious issues cannot be fed back to the leadership who may remain unaware of the depth and nature of those problems unless they become crises or scandals.

The intensity of the cycle of clergy family stress and a bishop's question at the end of the second session asking, 'What is the breaking point', led us to focus the third round of interviews on how the families knew when to seek help or take action, and if they didn't, when the breaking point of marriage or ministry might come. This might be a breakdown of physical or mental health, or a gradual deterioration of professional performance.

The interviews centred on four open questions. These looked first for positive experiences as well as exploring what might lead to a breaking point:

> What are you looking forward to most in the next five years?
> What would you be most concerned about in that time?

We then asked the children, the mother and then the father two further questions to allow the children and the mother to give their ideas without being influenced by the priest's reply:

> What would have to happen for your father to look for a new job?
> What would have to happen for him to look for a new job outside the ministry?

The catch-up session with the families again showed that they were very much in tune with one another's joys, achievements, and disappointments. In the next five years they were looking forward to all the normal experiences the children would face: starting school, changing schools, passing exams, achieving a variety of goals in sport, ballet, drama, music and other interests and preparing for a career.

For the parents, achieving goals in their current parishes was very important. New opportunities and responsibilities in their jobs, as well as training, mainly mentioned by wives, featured highly for the parents. Personal goals were much less prominent apart from special holidays, such as visiting family members who lived or worked abroad.

The same issues were also at the heart of their concerns: future plans that did not happen, failed exams, opportunities that did not arise, and goals that were not reached. Teenage children worried about moves. All but the youngest parents were concerned about the health and care of their own parents. Distance and restricted time off made it difficult to care for them. Even though the oldest vicar was only in his mid-40s, their own health, and the effects of the long-term demands of the job were a significant concern.

What would have to happen for the priest to look for a new job? Most families spoke of seeking God's guidance about when and why to move. The children again thought Dad might be offered a fabulous job by the bishop. If parents felt their task was complete in their present parish, they might explore a new challenge. Only one man talked of looking for a career move, although some implied this, but more in terms of a job that would stretch them rather than 'advancement'. One practical five-year-old thought, 'Dad would go down to the job centre'!

Equally, they spoke of negative situations that could motivate them to move: lack of diocesan or hierarchical support; laity promising support and commitment to spiritual and practical goals and 'not coming up with the goods', lack of commitment within a team; or boredom. The children talked about various problems: false accusations, massive revolt, people not trusting their Dad, or 'if everything fell apart'. There was concern that the end of a contract could mean a family had to move even if there was no other suitable job or a house to go to. Several expressed doubt about the whole appointments system and whether bishops really knew their clergy's competencies rather than simply wanting to fill vacancies. Most families said a new job would have to be right for all the family.

The overwhelming impression from all family members was that the priest would only leave the ministry for something 'very, very big' and 'severe'. One teenager spoke of her father as 'a priest forever'. Different theological issues were highlighted as reasons for leaving: the leadership denying key theological concepts like the Virgin birth or the Resurrection; ongoing issues around women's ordination; interfaith worship being held regularly in a church rather than a neutral setting, as Christian beliefs should be preached in a Christian building; and steps leading to homosexual marriage. These or any new doctrine or practice, which might deny an individual priest's beliefs, could lead them to leave the Church of England. However, they might look for ordination in another Christian denomination or a role with a charity or faith-based community where their commitment to ministry would continue.

The children were very down to earth about why the bishop might withdraw their father's license: scandal, father running off with the organist or mother with the churchwarden, raping choirboys, a hand in the till. Some couples said loss of faith would mean they could not go on. Four families specifically mentioned health breakdown as a reason, or advice not to continue in that post because of stress. If the wife died, several said the loss of practical, emotional and spiritual support might make parochial ministry impossible, especially with a family to care for.

Central to the discussion was the effect of disillusionment and frustration with the structures, or lack of structure and strategy within the Church. A man with a previous career of 12 years echoed others' concern that in the end the lack of 'support and reinforcement that you would have in a secular job' might 'get to me as I get older', giving 'a sense of no longer being able to cope'. There was also 'the constant wearing down process' from the general pressure of such a diffuse job 'without encouragement or feedback to know if it is aptly focused or a failure'. Days spent dealing with vandalism or acting as caretaker made vicars question the nature of the task.

Ultimately it would have to be something 'fairly disastrous' to motivate them to go through 'all that it means' to leave, so 'effectively you're trapped'. The couples spoke of having no house to go to. Some had no other professional training or knew their previous skills were outdated, so there would be no alternative job.

There was a tension between the cumulative effect of pressure and lack of support, and the fact that 'the older you get the harder it is to change'. It seemed that deep personal commitment led to the men continuing until something 'fairly disastrous' happened. Unless it was severe enough for the hierarchy to bring change, the difficulty of leaving a ministry that involved every aspect of the families' lives might mean they would remain.

In these interviews, the families mentioned five specific issues which they wanted the Church as an 'employing' organization to provide:

1. Clear strategy and structures with effective management.
2. Guidance to bring clarity to the task of ministry.
3. Support through communication and encouragement.
4. Ongoing training.
5. Stimulation to prevent boredom in the all-enveloping context of the job.

As the data show, the inherited structures, financial implications, resistance from some clergy to a more professional context, and bishops' impossible workload could all be stumbling blocks to addressing these issues.

II.   SUMMARY TO THE REFERENCE GROUPS

A conversation with a seven-year-old about her dinosaur collection, before one of the interviews began, seemed a helpful illustration of breakdown. She didn't think the dinosaurs had become extinct through a big bang causing a cloud of dust but through rodents eating their eggs, causing a gradual decline to extinction.

Based on this conversation and her favourite dinosaur, 'Dipplydocus', we sent a single summary after the third interviews to both the Reference Groups. In brief this said:

What became of 'Dipplydocus' – A Profile and a Process of Vulnerability

1. Is there a 'breaking point'?

One of the more senior research clergy had a breakdown and subsequent relief from duty for several months between the second and third interviews. This appeared to have come out of the blue, until he looked back on his work schedule over a period of time and wondered how he had lasted so long. There were many parallels with his situation for the other research families as they approached the same stage of ministry.

2. Profile of vulnerability

In our summary to the Groups after the third interviews, we outlined indicators of stress highlighted by the families. These may have accumulated over long periods of time. They might go unnoticed by the leadership or even by clergy themselves unless explored in supervision or consultation. They may come when a priest has little or no time for professional and personal development or recreation, or when he has additional responsibility at diocesan level. High ideals will mean he does not stint himself in the job. The heart of the problem may lie around the diffuse boundary between the clergyman's work and his family life.

3. The process

The wearing-down process seemed to be linked to both positive and negative aspects of the job being carried into the family. They are expected, and usually expect themselves, to demonstrate an ideal of belief, commitment and family life. Concern to live up to this ideal leads families to share the positives and absorb the negatives, even though these negatives may belong to the wider church or to society as a whole. Encouragement tends to be given for work well done rather than for burdens courageously carried. This adds to the tendency to highlight the positives and deny the negatives. The Accommodation Syndrome then comes into play.

4. Conclusion

The process, if allowed to operate, may lead to long-term deterioration of the priest's ministry or possibly breakdown of ministry on a temporary or permanent basis. This is costly to the Church and devastating to the family. It may be hard for the leadership, the laity and possibly many clergy, their partners and their children, to recognize the process and find a less idealistic and more natural way of approaching ministry.

PART SIX
Responses and
Conclusions

18 The Response of the Groups

I. THE PASTORAL GROUP'S RESPONSE

The Pastoral Group's discussion of the summary we had sent them of the third interviews highlighted three main concerns:

1. The seriousness of the problems the Group members were encountering.
2. The significant variation from diocese to diocese in the way problems were handled.
3. The tendency of the hierarchy to cover up problems, which often meant they were not addressed, or only addressed when a problem became a crisis.

The Group spoke first of breakdown and deterioration of ministry and reiterated their concern for strict confidentiality as they were speaking of actual cases. The discussion centred mainly around marriage breakdown rather than breakdown of ministry.

The Group felt that, at times, diocesan bishops could handle difficult situations well, and examples were given such as the parish and marriage situation being restored following a priest's affair. The fact that a priest was in public life nevertheless made it difficult for 'mistakes' to be forgotten. In several other instances the Group felt the main concern of the hierarchy was that the problem should be 'hushed up'. Small indications of difficulty, 'cries for help', went unrecognized and support and help were seldom offered, or not until more severe symptoms became evident. Clergy themselves became very good at covering up what was happening until the marriage or ongoing ministry was irretrievable.

They said that as the hierarchy were not in close touch with clergy, difficulties could be repeated and there could be more than one affair or an affair could continue, although the priest might deny this. Again examples were given.

Five potential hazards were mentioned, some touched on previously:

- The priest could feel professionally isolated and generally cut off if his wife was working, especially if he was the only professional in an inner city area, on a housing estate or left in the country in a 'dormitory' village.
- The ideal of love and closeness could lead to the crossing of sexual boundaries, especially as much of a vicar's work takes place with individuals or small groups. Clergy who offered ongoing counselling might not have the supervision considered essential within professional counselling guidelines. This crossing of boundaries might be linked to their need of affirmation. If the hierarchy did not give affirmation, it might be sought or welcomed on a more personal level.
- They thought there could also be a confusion of sexual identity for male clergy who are asked to wear flowing clerical dress and express traits often considered as feminine, but at the same time may be addressed as 'Father'. Clergy or a clergy couple might have a sense of separation from everyday reality, particularly when people look to the figurehead and the role rather than to the person.
- One member suggested that those who might have a homosexual orientation could feel pressure to marry and become 'a vicarage family', which would lead to marriage difficulties. This echoed an article in the *Guardian* (30 November 1992) by The Rev. Malcolm Johnson who at that time convened the Gay Clergy Group in London.
- The Pastoral Group thought the previous strong taboo against clergy divorce meant marriage breakdown was seen to be more likely among older clergy. They considered new patterns of independence within partnerships, and different expectations of joint responsibility for the home and children, now meant that younger clergy couples were seeking help in more of a discussion context.

II. THE LEADERSHIP GROUP'S RESPONSE

The work with the families to date was briefly summarized for the Leadership Group. We reported the concern of the Pastoral Group over issues they were facing with clergy and their families. We said that the convenors of supervision groups for clergy counsellors with whom we had been in touch were 'shell shocked' by the severity of the problems encountered by counsellors. One member asked, 'Is the crisis growing?' and 'Is there a movement in one direction?'

We said the interviews all showed why it was difficult for families to talk about the negatives, so the extent and direction of 'the crisis' could only be judged by indicators rather than be defined. In response to the Dipplydocus paper, the Leadership Group discussed concerns and problems they experienced in relation to these issues. Again their focus was more on the priests' ministry than on family issues, and possibly more on solving or minimizing the public impact of problems than on the problems themselves, their origins and preventive measures.

I. Affairs

At times the Leadership Group seemed very uncertain as they addressed issues such as affairs of priests, especially as a priest might have had not one, but two or three affairs. One member mentioned a 'horrendous case' of several affairs after which the priest attempted suicide, and asked, 'What do you do?' The underlying issues that might lead to an affair were only touched on in their discussion. Another member then asked 'What is our problem?' Several difficulties for the Leadership were discussed and seemed to centre on four factors: lack of finance, lack of time, lack of experience in handling such issues, and the need for damage limitation to the image of the Church.

The Group said that bishops do not have the finance to deal with cases. If, as a result of their behaviour, clergy are removed from a stipendiary post, they go with uncertain support. Cases are assessed individually, and finance and housing assistance provided for the family depending on funding available in that diocese. Help is mostly given by the Clergy Charities.

They felt that Senior Staff Meetings were not taking enough time and trouble to ensure that clergy facing problems were put in the way of help. There were many different models for dealing with such situations. The priest might be 'shifted' to another diocese. Some bishops would say that they would accept X if the other diocese would accept Y. This might work if the entire background was known and there was supervision. Some felt a new start in another area should be monitored and would expect feedback. One comment was that the leadership was not good at 'following up sadness'. Some were afraid of intruding or taking a firm line, although the Group felt that they should. They said there were bishops who felt they had a vocation to accept anybody, and allow them to rebuild their lives. A member who asked if this was public knowledge was told that it was known in certain circles.

There was no system of middle management to address the problem. They said that area/rural deans had a heavy caseload in their deanery as well as their parish. If problems received media coverage or became known to the public it could be more difficult to find solutions.

The Leadership Group were perplexed about how to deal with clergy partners who had an affair. Leaders had no specific jurisdiction in relation to partners, but an affair undercut the ideal of family life, and inevitably had an impact on the image of the church as a whole. Some of the issues mentioned by the Group would now come under the 2003 Disciplinary Measure, although not in relation to partners.

2. Individual finance

The Group's discussion again focused on the demands made by those who got into financial difficulties rather than considering the reasons why debt might be incurred and how training in financial planning could help. Sometimes personal debts would be paid two or three times. If a man needed help every six months, experts would be sent in. A case was mentioned where a Rural Dean was visiting a priest every month to monitor his financial management. Another priest was sent on a financial management course.

The Group were conscious of the stipend providing a minimal level of income, but they might not have access to both husband and wife to discuss financial management. They thought those who were ordained from a successful, well-rewarded situation were coming into a very different lifestyle, and might have a sense that the Church 'owed' them good living conditions, especially in terms of housing.

3. Church finance

Two challenges were highlighted by the Group which are changing the present patterns of ministry. First, the financial crisis within the church as a whole would affect the pattern of stipendiary ministry. Recruitment, vocation and the 'job shape' for clergy in the world of the twenty-first century needed to be looked at carefully. One member suggested that there would be fewer clergy, more hierarchy, more mobility and more need for pastoral care. They did not expand on how mobility might affect families.

Second, parishes now have to find the majority of the money for clergy stipends through the quota system. Over time this will give a different clergy/laity balance. Laity may require clergy to undertake certain tasks, either practical or spiritual, because congregations are responsible for paying them. Under previous funding methods there was more leeway for individual priests to decide how to exercise their ministry.

4. Appointments and references

Group Members felt that job interviews have an element of competitiveness and raise hopes, which for three out of four candidates are not fulfilled. They asked, 'How do those not selected cope with the rejection?' The two American research projects described in Chapter 4 recommended debriefing for candidates.

The interviews showed that all the family put much emotional energy and thought into applications, so debriefing could be an important support for the leadership to initiate. Procedures for making senior appointments, including suffragan bishops and canons, were described as 'very odd'.

The Leadership Group's discussion about references was linked to that on appointments and showed concerns about how to deal with candidates for ordination or for new posts who were known to have problems. Several significant points were raised:

- The Group were aware of the danger of references being read in different ways. They fell into two categories: one was positive, because some referees would never say anything negative; the other gave 'a fuller picture', but some people reacted against these. It was then a question of reading codes. One Group member said he had only just realized the problem of different types of reference and different attitudes and responses to them.
- The purpose of a reference was raised, asking if it was seen as a

reference or a commendation. Equally, were referees acting for the bishop, for the clergy, or for the benefit of the church at large?

- College staff members were given guidelines for references. College principals and sometimes bishops had to share these with candidates. If candidates also signed the references, these could be bland and were then hard to write, especially if there were doubts about the student/priest. Principals might not deal with sensitive issues in a report but might ring up the bishop. Equally bishop might ring bishop.
- There was also a question of confidentiality. The candidate might tell the bishop or principal that if certain information were shared he would fail in his application. Equally, bishops sometimes left out significant details like a very large debt, although some might own up.
- One member said that, unlike some interviewers, he sometimes challenged the referee and discovered information at a selection conference or an interview that might not come out otherwise. He would ask if this could be shared with the bishop. If the answer was no, the candidate's name would not be included in the general circulation of priests who were looking for new appointments.

5. Ambition

There was uncertainty and ambivalence among clergy around the whole subject of ambition. The Leadership Group's discussion reflected these same attitudes and different views were expressed. Comments were made that clergy were competitive and ambitious but not allowed to be seen as such. They were trained as servants of the Lord and also taught that the vital thing was self-value.

We asked the Group how clergy should distinguish between a concern to value and use their talents, on the one hand, and ambition on the other. This distinction was not directly addressed. Two comments linked with this: the issue was about seeking help and admitting if someone was ambitious, and an Episcopal review helping clergy to do what they do better, but not being an evaluation. They said that post-ordination training conferences considered career structure and ambition, so these were now addressed at an early stage. One member said that ambitious clergy could be picked out in six months. Some younger clergy thought ambition was unacceptable but there were also people being ordained from other professions who possibly had different perceptions.

6. Children

They felt it mattered to children if their parent was moved on and appreciated. The Group said that in business, status is contextualized and children could feel proud of their parents, but priests' children feel marginalized. A priest's self-value is low and their family feels that. This linked to a point in The Cornerstone Project, outlined in Chapter 4, that the clergy role had changed from high status and low stress to low status and high stress.

Several other comments were made about children. One member said it was amazing if children remain faithful to Christ because their experience of being in a clergy family was so varied. Two members said their children had experienced hell through school but real warmth in the parish. If a vicar was trying to move his parish forward and there was resistance, his wife and children could have hassle from the parish, or from the incumbent himself, because of the pressure. If, in the future, the parish were responsible for paying the whole of the stipend, it would change the balance and the hassle could increase.

The Group thought that parishes did not view other problems in clergy families sympathetically. The families themselves did not want to talk about the 'darkness' in their family and there was often a cover up. What was shared varied from family to family. Promises made at the point of ordination were OK while children were little, but at a later stage there could be family expectations of children. There could be pressure on parents, which caused division, if children adopted secular values and 'shacked up'. It was suggested that this affected 'an enormous percentage'. They thought that despite the pressures, clergy still wanted their children to be ordained and that a high proportion of ordinands are clergy children, although they did not give the factual basis for these observations.

7. Support

The Group felt that clergy families in need of support should feel free to contact the leadership at an early stage, and time should be found for them, rather than referring them on too easily to a consultant. Some bishops, and sometimes their wives, visited clergy regularly as well as praying for them. Support groups for bishops were seen as modelling a general need for support. Use of centres like the Society of Mary and Martha, mentioned in Chapter 4, I, should be normal and acceptable. One member asked if a bishop who had been in post for 20 years could understand the current problems clergy were facing, again the suggestion of a generational divide.

III. REFLECTIONS ON THE GROUPS' RESPONSES

The Pastoral Group members were very aware of the problems faced by clergy and their families and of some of the underlying causes. Their discussion suggested that no one within diocesan structures was close enough to clergy or their families to pick up early warning signs or cries for help. These might, therefore, go unrecognized, or potential problems might be hushed up unless or until a crisis occurred. The Group's comments showed the importance of counselling being available. They recommended that supervision or consultation should be provided as a means of supporting clergy in their ministry.

The issues underlying the Leadership Group's discussion were those of policy and management. Their comments show that policy is decided within individual dioceses and according to the particular beliefs and training of individual bishops, archdeacons and even rural deans.

Their response suggested there was pressure to deal with problems with a minimum of time and expense. If senior leaders are only seeing crises, their perspective on problems will be unbalanced. As counselling and support are separated from the leadership, they are distanced from the general issues of clergy family stress. Individuals in the hierarchy may be aware of specific issues that could lead to difficulties for the families, but their primary focus seemed to be on the ability of clergy to cope.

The research was considering stress for clergy *families* rather than just for priests. Nevertheless, reduced stress for priests would be a considerable step in reducing stress for clergy families. The 2003 Disciplinary Measure not only gives guidelines for the behaviour of priests but also holds bishops responsible for their decisions in dealing with problems across the range of difficulties. They may now be asked to account for actions they have taken over particular priests, for example, in cases of sexual abuse.

The impact of the Disciplinary Measure was highlighted by The Bishop of Southwark, The Rt Rev Tom Butler, in an article in the *Guardian* on 10 June, 2006. 'Traditionally clergy both see themselves as answerable to their bishop and look to their bishop for direction, support and pastoral care. The form that this accountability and support takes is dramatically changing at the moment. We are on the cusp between that which is no longer effective, and that which has not yet been invented. This is not a comfortable place to be.'

Members of the Leadership Group could be considered to be more in tune with the issues, and certainly as concerned about them as most other members of the hierarchy, by the fact that they were prepared to set aside so much time to consider them for the research. Nevertheless they were still asking fundamental questions about how the whole subject of clergy family stress could be dealt with, rather than suggesting strategies to discover why these problems were there and how to address them.

For the clergy themselves, the questions at the heart of the second round of interviews were, 'What is the task of the priest?' and 'Is the church working to a model of ministry?' The third round of interviews indirectly raised the questions, 'What is the task of the leadership?' and 'Are they working to a model of management?'

The pressing leadership tasks, in the opinion of all three levels of the Church addressed by the research, seem to be:

- To provide clear structures for ministry and pastoral care of clergy families;
- To provide effective management, training and monitoring in order to prevent the breakdown or reduced effectiveness of such ministry, or other serious problems.

The difficulty of addressing these issues in a systematic way and of providing management training were highlighted after a letter to the *Church Times* (17 October 1997) from an archdeacon, commenting on his university diploma in company direction. This provoked some in-depth comment, a week later. The first letter said:

'Far too often those in authority are reluctant to use the abilities of its priests and people. My experience, having left a large international corporation to be ordained, after 20 years as a senior executive, was that, together with other students in similar positions, I was subjected to a de-skilling process at theological college.

'In my parish there are a number of highly-skilled and senior lay people from all walks of life at the top in their particular disciplines. Instead of sending people on courses, we should be big enough to use the talents available.'

A second clergyman recommended The Open University's six-month course, Managing Voluntary and Non-Profit Enterprises, as 'management skills are not instinctive, nor are they conferred with the grace of orders ...'

Another, from The Centre for Voluntary Organizations at the London School of Economics, asked,

'Which is the most appropriate model and training for the management of the Church of England? The Church is more like a network of voluntary organizations. Models developed through studying them have been fruitfully applied to religious organizations.'

The Convenor of the Management for Ministry MSc and Diploma at Roehampton Institute found that,

'For course members, their pastoral, teaching and training roles are enhanced through deep and theologically aware study of management disciplines, including general management and more specialized people-, finance-, and marketing-management skills.'

The current situation may reflect the polarization between a 'business model' and a 'spiritual model' outlined by the Pastoral Group and confirmed by the Leadership Group. Both the data and the letters suggest that for some leaders the spiritual model implies discarding, ignoring or denying previous skills of older ordinands, as well as 'those at the top of their discipline'. The rich training resources that they could provide are then lost to the Church.

There are huge complexities in running a diocese or a large team in the twenty-first century. If those who are appointed to such leadership positions have not had specific preparation at each stage of their ministry, they may face the additional stress of training on the job.

The many questions raised by the Leadership Group also suggested that uncertainty itself is part of their pressure. If there was clear communication to clergy families about the appropriate place to discuss each of the issues they faced, it would provide great support to them, and also free bishops and archdeacons from many day-to-day queries and interruptions.

The questions in the third interviews focused on how the families would know when to seek help, and if they didn't, what was the breaking point? As few, if any, members of diocesan staff are close to clergy, and probably even less in touch with clergy families, they are unlikely to be aware of issues they have to cope with. Parish leaders may leave difficulties of which they are aware until they are severe before mentioning them to the bishop. Clergy and their families are aware of problems reflecting on their job, so again may hesitate to seek help.

Consultation and clearer structures for pastoral care would make it less likely that parish issues or personal problems could remain hidden. Breakdown in marriage or ministry would then be far less likely to come 'out of the blue' as workloads would be regularly reviewed. Any 'day-to-day safety net' would make access to general support much more accessible to both clergy and their families before difficulties became crises.

19 Reflections and Dilemmas

I.   INTRODUCTION

Like all stories, rabbi, priest and vicar tales can be read at different levels of meaning. In one that helps to illustrate the dilemmas of clergy families and the Church, the rabbi, priest and vicar go fishing. Shortly after anchoring, the rabbi remembers that he has left his bait on the shore, steps out of the boat, walks across the water's surface and returns the same way, rucksack in hand. Some time later, the priest realizes that his sandwiches are in the car. He, in turn, climbs over the side of the dinghy, walks across the water and returns with his lunch.

The vicar, feeling the pressure to show similar faith, says he must fetch an extra jumper, steps over the gunwale and sinks like a stone. The priest turns to the rabbi. 'Do you think we should have told him where the causeway is?'

It is helpful to put this story alongside the central themes of this book which have been:

The need for good communication.
Respect and support for those 'employed' by the organization.
Affirmation of their strengths and resources.
Appropriate discussion and guidance in focusing their job.
Acknowledgement of work-related difficulties which clergy and their families face in their unique circumstances.
Discussion of the changes in Church structures that would address the dilemmas raised by the Groups and the families.

The questions around communication in the story would include not only where the causeway is, but also broader issues: whether anyone has thought to build a causeway in the first place, how sound it is, where the potholes are, whether it can be used only at certain states of the tide and how much time could be saved by swimming direct to the specific point on the beach. The underlying principle is that, given all the information, the vicar could make his own decisions. He would not feel he had to act to prove a point, or be unnecessarily diverted from the task in hand, but could use his energies in more constructive ways, such as catching fish! Equally, if his family knew the information was available, they could plan their lives in a different way.

Alternatively, the vicar and his family could, of course, be given the number of the lifeboat station to programme into their mobile phones in case of emergencies, a cure as opposed to prevention.

Analogies are always limited, but the story can help us to think about the whole picture for clergy families.

Three factors were striking during the final review of all that the families and Groups had said.

1. *Commitment* The degree of commitment to their faith and ministry of all those involved in the research at every level.
2. *Questions* The number of questions raised by the Reference Groups, and particularly the Leadership Group, in relation to clergy families and how few answers, if any, they had to the issues these highlighted, despite their obvious deep concern.
3. *Comparisons* Most striking of all were the many comparisons made by members of the Groups throughout the research. These included comparisons between: clergy and other professions; clergy and the leadership; clergy and laity; clergy and other clergy; clergy and their wives; the vows of ordination and the vows of marriage; success and failure. Comparisons were also made between families of the laity or the general public and clergy families, such as whether clergy families were more able to achieve an ideal of family life, itself almost always undefined; the achievement of clergy children compared with others; possessions; and the ability to cope.

More subtle comparisons or polarizations were also made:

1. If clergy followed a 'business model' of ministry rather than an ascetic model they would be 'missing out on holiness'.
2. If clergy were not independent, even in circumstances where independent action was not possible, they were seen as emotionally dependent.

3. If clergy were not able to find solutions to issues on which they had been given no guidance, or that were the responsibility of other parts of the diocese or parish, they were seen to be inept or lacking initiative and determination.
4. If they were not 'successful' in terms of ecclesiastical advancement, they were often categorized as 'failing'.
5. The need for supervision or work consultancy, considered essential in other caring professions and increasingly in all professions, was also seen as an inability to cope.

A fundamental statement, explored in the discussion of methodology, was that the 'unique and specific context of a situation' must be examined, as situations may have many similarities, but also significant differences. Any comparison diverts attention away from the situation being researched and denies its 'unique and specific context'. The nature of the comparisons noted above suggest a deep denial of the validity of the clergy families' perspective, because this perspective is not being assessed in itself, but weighed against the situation of others. Two factors are involved. One is the need for a realistic assessment of the demands and dilemmas in this particular profession, which may lead to confusion or difficulties for the individual or family. The other is that the conflicting demands necessitate a 'both/and' perspective rather than an 'either/or' approach.

For instance, the lack of clear structures within the church frustrates both bishops and clergy although it affects them in different ways. Bishops have a responsibility towards both clergy and laity although their needs may be different. Professionalism and an ascetic model of ministry could be integrated. 'Success' should be seen in a much broader context. Clergy may have found it hard to reach specific goals because of unforeseeable obstacles, but may have achieved other, possibly more realistic goals. They may have influenced a smaller number of people but at a more profound level. A comparative, conflictual stance can be destructive, and in the situation of clergy families can only create and maintain stress.

This sense of constant comparison and the way it diverts attention from the situation of clergy families is an underlying theme of the conclusions drawn from the research.

II. THE 'STORYLINE' OR THE UNIFYING THEME OF THE RESEARCH

We used the social science method of Grounded Theory (see Chapter 6 III) to analyse all the information we received. The final stage of this is to look for links between all sources to find a unifying theme – the 'storyline' of the research. So what is the storyline concerning stress experienced by clergy families, and the response of the Church of England as an organization?

The first striking factor, causing significant stress to both bishops and clergy, is that the Church of England operates within widely fragmented structures. Once the Church of England became the Established Church, the State held considerable power. Political as well as spiritual considerations then influenced policy, both nationally and in each diocese. The resulting inherited systems have many anomalies, such as patronage, the ongoing influence of the freehold, and the independence of each diocese. One bishop aptly described the current position as '42 dioceses, each with 200 or more corner shops'.

Bishops, archdeacons, clergy and laity all struggle with these existing structures. This fragmentation and variation leaves the leadership with a sense that no one is in control, no one has clear authority, and there is no clarity in relation to procedures. Examples included different bishops having different approaches to the way they deal with references, clergy problems and any restrictions they might impose, although guidelines under the 2003 Disciplinary Measure have helped to bring a more even approach.

These unclear procedures leave clergy uncertain of appropriate action in many fields. They have infrequent personal contact with the leadership apart from Episcopal reviews. Bishops spoke of their own support groups as a model but clergy mentioned only occasional reviews with clergy peers. Clergy had little opportunity to discuss current issues or future directions because regular supervision was not provided. As a result their families became their main 'professional' support.

Personal concerns for clergy and their families could be discussed with counsellors. The leadership do not know whether church structures support these concerns, or are partly responsible for them, because of the confidentiality of counselling. They may only see situations that become crises or scandals. The data suggest that what they do not see is the ongoing competent coping of clergy and families with many challenging and difficult issues.

As a result, the hierarchy expressed concern that clergy and their families are dependent instead of independent. Independence, however, needs to be underpinned by a Secure Base with good communication and support, as shown in Chapter 12, in order for clergy 'to press forward and take risks'.

The Church does not appear to have generally agreed operational policies in relation to the nature of the task of ministry, training, and professional/personal boundaries among other issues. Clergy independence then has an uncertain foundation. Where policies or guidelines exist these may be implemented very differently from diocese to diocese.

The general uncertainly affects the families too. The literature showed that healthy functioning in both families *and* organizations is promoted by stability, consistency, clarity and flexibility of structures, effective leadership, support and communication. If these factors are largely uncertain or absent in the functioning of the Church as an organization, this must undermine healthy functioning of clergy families within it.

In addition, clergy families are on the front line in representing the Christian faith to the wider community. We have seen that there are particular pressures on all those whose work is carried out as public figures. For clergy, their role brings many varied expectations from both congregations and the public. This is increased by the Church of England being the Established Church, with clergy having a responsibility towards everyone in the parish, not only church members.

A particular expectation, also expressed formally at ordination, is that the families of clergy will live out a Christian ideal of family life. In contrast, every message, overt and covert, from all levels of the Church is that the job must have priority. The job has few boundaries and may entail a three-session day, six days a week, and a sense that the job is never finished. This makes it very difficult to set aside time for the family. The expectation to show the ideal in both the job and the family then becomes contradictory, catching clergy families in a Double Bind.

The families tended to respond to this Double Bind by accommodating to the situation, because of potential loss for themselves and the church 'family' if they challenged the contradiction. As the family live in tied housing and will usually share the ideal, they have a high investment in the job being a 'success'.

Consequently, clergy families are drawn in to support the clergy job and to relieve pressure on the priest. The stresses of the job are then taken back into the family and may cause family conflict.

The Leadership Group spoke of not taking time to attend to 'cries for help' from clergy or families because of the pressure of their own task. For the same reason, little time was given to discussion of pastoral issues for clergy and their families. It seemed that both professional and pastoral isolation meant that clergy families are left to cope alone with stress with little support.

We saw in the Double ABCX model in Chapter 5 how crisis can develop when stress accumulates, leading to a 'pile-up in the family system'.. This may mean that efforts to master a situation are unsuccessful, as shown by the breakdown of an able priest before the third interview. An alternative pattern is that clergy will experience ennui and withdraw.

One particular source of stress is that 'the unique and specific context' within which clergy live and work is not acknowledged, and clergy families are compared with those of other professions or families. The additional pressures of wider family issues or life cycle stages in the church or in the family are often not recognized.

III. DILEMMAS

As well as these organizational issues, which affected all sections of the Church in various ways, there were specific dilemmas for each level that had taken part in the research. We shall also consider how these relate to the overall dilemma outlined in Chapter 1, 'Why does the Church, part of whose purpose is to care for others, seem to find it so hard to care for its carers?'

1. Dilemmas for clergy and clergy families

1. *A clergy family voice*

The greatest dilemma for clergy and their families was that there was no appropriate place in the Church of England where their concerns could be heard in a calm, non-confrontational context. This was one factor leading to a widespread sense of isolation and stress.

2. Commitment, the freehold, and dependency

Both Groups said throughout that they wished clergy would be more independent. The data showed that once clergy had spent five or six years in theological training and a curacy they were unlikely to be qualified for their previous jobs in a fast moving, technological age. They had lived on minimal income in tied housing during that period, so in many areas of professional and family life they had become dependent on the Church.

This dependency will be more insecure in the future as the removal of the freehold will mean all new clergy appointments will be for a fixed term. The family, however, will still be required to live in the house provided as a condition of service. Throughout the interviews all family members discussed the wide range of professional and personal factors which might make a move necessary. Clergy children were acutely aware of the risk of living on the job if that job failed.

This aspect of their dependent position did not appear to be acknowledged by the Reference Groups, particularly the Leadership Group, in their wish for clergy to be more independent. According to the data, the families' expectation that *their* commitment would be reflected in a reciprocal commitment from the Church generally was almost always unrealized.

3. The need for definition of the clergy task

A central theme of the second interviews, at all three levels, was that the clergy task is undefined. Much time and concern were spent on this dilemma. As Handy points out in The Doughnut Principle in Chapter 12, III, there are few core tasks for clergy but endless options beyond those tasks with no clear professional boundaries. Clergy are therefore one of the groups most likely to suffer stress.

The Leadership Group suggested that rural deans, post-ordination training and colleagues could all help clergy with guidance on this issue, but most of these 'support systems' varied greatly and could be intermittent or ineffective.

4. A Secure Base: support, consultation, training and stimulation

The importance of a Secure Base underpins all the dilemmas faced by clergy and their families.

The majority of clergy stated or implied that the absence of adequate professional support, regular appraisal and consultation could lead them in time to consider leaving the ministry. References to training were significantly lacking in the interviews, although some of the clergy had been ordained for 15 to 20 years. Lack of contact with the leadership and other clergy led to a lack of affirmation. Their deep sense of isolation and almost total lack of stimulation added to anxiety for both clergy and the families about the effects of long-term ministry.

5. Expectations

Clergy and their families face a constant range of expectations expressed in many and varied ways. Bentham's concept of the Panopticon in Chapter 14, I clearly illustrates the effects of people never knowing when they are being observed, which all members of the family felt. This caused children in particular to be both uncertain and angry if they were watched and criticised unfairly.

6. Isolation from extended family and the community

The families found contact with extended family and friends was scant because of distance and lack of free time. The size of curates' houses meant it was very difficult for them to have visitors. Support to and from grandparents was therefore reduced. The physical isolation of many clergy houses compounded the families' general sense of isolation.

7. Health

A particular area of concern for the families was the long-term effect of persistent stress on the health of all members. The issues described in the sections on Health in Chapters 7, II, and 15, III, show the extent of stress-related illness in the families, which was often unknown to the leadership or to congregations. Even when the family appeared to be functioning well, within the parameters of healthy family functioning generally, there could still be hidden stress, possibly leading to dysfunction, because of the uncertainty of the job.

The models of stress in Chapter 5 showed that this could be reduced if a person has some sense of control, even when faced with extremely difficult situations. The sense of the families frequently having little control was shown throughout the interviews.

8. A longer time frame

Problems the families faced were viewed by others in a short-term perspective or with only one aspect being considered, rather than these being seen in the long term for the families as a whole and in a wider perspective. This perspective would include all the issues discussed in this chapter.

2. Dilemmas for those responsible for pastoral care

It seemed that pastoral carers within the Church are working in a vacuum. As the Leadership Group said, responsibility for pastoral care is being left with counsellors and others appointed by the leadership. This raised three particular dilemmas:

1. Confidentiality

The first is that counsellors work under a professional code of conduct, which entails complete confidentiality between the counsellor and the client unless there is risk of injury to others or self-harm. Counsellors therefore carry responsibility for all the issues that clergy and their families bring to them, as they cannot feed back difficulties to the leadership without the permission of the priest and/ or the family. As the Leadership Group acknowledged, this leaves an unfair weight of responsibility on counsellors. One bishop raised the question, 'Who is solving the problem?'

2. Professional responsibility

The second is the confusion between the provision of counselling and pastoral care on a personal level, and other support systems. Other systems in a professional context may include spiritual direction, work consultancy, supervision and Episcopal review. If counselling is thought by some of the leadership to cover all areas apart from Episcopal review, this implies a significant confusion of professional and personal boundaries.

3. Serious issues

Both Reference Groups suggested that if the extent of the very serious issues of inappropriate behaviour, debt, ennui and other problems were more generally known, there would be a much greater concern by church members and the hierarchy to address issues of stress for clergy and their families. Currently, however, unless such issues reach the public domain, counsellors continue to carry the burden.

3. Dilemmas for the leadership

The Leadership faced a series of dilemmas in responding to the issues raised by clergy families in the research.

1. Pressure of the job and expectations of the leadership
It was obvious from all the Leadership Group said that they faced an enormous task in leading the Church of England as an organization and as a spiritual force. They spoke of diaries permanently full with appointments across the spectrum of duties. The pressure of time on the leadership is a significant factor in the operation of the whole system of the church as an organization. The Group mentioned the need for more bishops during their discussions.

Bishops and archdeacons are also the focus of many expectations from all levels of society, particularly the expectation that they would have the answers to wider questions within the Church. The Doughnut Principle, outlined in Chapter 12, applied to the leadership as much as it did to parish clergy.

2. Training
Ongoing learning at every level is emphasized in current thinking on healthy organizations but the data suggested that training and ongoing learning for clergy is sparse at each stage. Even senior leaders may then have to learn their tasks of leadership and management once they are in post, with little or no specific preparatory training.

3. Structures and areas of responsibility
The Storyline in II above shows that the church struggles with unclear and inconsistent structures at all levels which links to historical factors and the ongoing relationship of Church and State. The structures themselves could be applied differently in different dioceses. This led the Leadership Group to say that 'no one has authority'. However, clergy, the wider Church or the general public think the leadership does have authority, and do not realize that this authority is frequently proscribed by the system. This is especially so as clergy are given authority at ordination by the bishop and instituted into their parishes under the bishop's authority.

Delegated authority needs clear and consistent structures with feedback. If the leadership feels that their authority is uncertain, this uncertainty will be reflected and magnified in any delegated authority. It will also be reflected in how the Church's professional responsibility for clergy and their families is organized. In particular, if delegated responsibility, such as organizing clergy housing, has no structure for appropriate oversight and feedback, the leadership will not know if this delegated responsibility has been accepted and adequately fulfilled.

4. References
The Leadership Group said there was no common understanding about the focus of a reference and these were handled in a very individual way. There were guidelines for college staff and principals but not, it seemed, for the leadership. Even when references are agreed and signed by both parties, additional information might be given verbally without the applicant's knowledge.

5. Addressing the families' needs
We have seen the number of questions and dilemmas the Leadership Group raised about clergy and clergy families. There was no indication that members of the Group or other leaders had discussed these issues previously with clergy or clergy families. As a result, the issues seem to be addressed according to individual perspectives in individual dioceses, rather than with some degree of consensus. Some of the questions remain unanswered.

All the dilemmas contribute to the overall dilemma of the Church finding it so hard to care for its carers. We have seen how clergy and their families experience the Double Bind in fundamental ways. Unless the dilemmas are addressed, the Church is leaving clergy to bear their responsibility using their own spiritual and practical resources, and to find solutions to difficulties largely on their own. The resulting stress is borne primarily by the families.

20 Recommendations

I. ADDRESSING THE DILEMMAS

The financial, sociological and spiritual situation of society at this stage of the early twenty-first century is changing rapidly, raising new issues as well as intensifying existing ones. The Church is changing too and already, in a series of ways, it has begun to address some of the issues raised in the book, but still the dilemmas remain.

The diminishing number of priests will mean a gradual shift of emphasis to greater lay leadership in parishes and to clergy who will train laity. This points to a new 'wholeness' of ministry with a better-trained core of able laity, and a mission to the whole community from all members of local congregations.

With so much change, it would be easy for the ongoing dilemmas and contradictions highlighted in this research to be overlooked. The pressures from unclear structures, unrealistic expectations and the health risks of overwork will then continue unchanged. Clergy marriages will continue to be at risk. Clergy children will continue to be vulnerable. There will still be a pressing need for an integrated theology of the married priesthood.

Our recommendations are based on the many potential 'solutions' suggested in the interviews and Group discussions, and should be read in conjunction with the dilemmas outlined in Chapter 19.

1. The clergy task

The issues of the clergy task and management raised by all three levels of the Church involved in the research are summarized in Chapter 18 III.

• The leadership task

Discussion between bishops, between bishops and archdeacons, and with others in leadership positions helps to achieve consensus about their roles. This could protect different members of the leadership from an impossible workload by a clearer definition of their responsibilities. Setting out issues that they would *not* normally address, and establishing other means for these to be dealt with, could give bishops and archdeacons space to exercise their key roles without unnecessary diversions.

● **The clergy task**

The absence of a 'job description' meant clergy as well as the leadership found it hard to know how to deal with the many demands on them and how to focus their task. As a result they faced endless expectations, which intruded on their time and energy as well as their family life.

If the leadership were to set out the core tasks for clergy as well as for themselves, and also those issues and tasks that are seen as the responsibility of the laity, it would bring clarity to the task at all levels of ministry. Wide-ranging discussion on the nature of the task of parish clergy and models of ministry could explore different options and approaches for clergy and parishes to consider. This could encompass the many and varied aspects of such a broad Church. It would also address the idea, still widely held, that clergy are the ones who 'do ministry properly'.

The fact that these issues would be articulated and discussed could begin to address the hidden nature and confusion of the Double Bind for clergy, and so release their families from providing 'professional' support.

2. Ongoing training

Ongoing in-service training for clergy in line with other caring professions could address many dilemmas. Initial training in dealing with administrative tasks could lift pressure for clergy at each stage as so many clergy struggle with this issue. Most professions require their members to attend three or four workshops or conferences a year if they are to maintain their registration. They are expected to conduct their work with personal integrity, and to keep up to date with developing professional ideas and information. By providing a service of the highest quality, working within the disciplines of their profession, they show respect for those they serve, and earn the confidence of their clients.

This is as true for clergy as for other professionals. They, too, are expected to work within professional standards of conduct as they deal with many people who may be vulnerable or at key stages in their lives. In addition their conduct of regular worship and weddings, baptisms and funerals can enrich people's lives and give them confidence and spiritual support at times of major personal and family change.

Ongoing training provides protection for congregations and the general public. This is not always emphasized sufficiently. If clergy are to maintain standards of the highest quality in their demanding vocation, training needs to be seen as a necessity rather than an optional extra. Historically the independence of the freehold has made training hard to enforce. At this moment, when fundamental changes in terms and conditions of service and the freehold are being established, there could be an opportunity to address concerns of both clergy and the leadership by grasping the nettle of obligatory in-service training.

Clergy who took part in training during the research indicated that it brought stimulation, a great reduction in isolation, a fresh focus to the job and a new sense of competence. The data showed that clergy coming into ministry from a previous job found it much harder to work without the regular training and appraisal that had been such a central part of their previous experience.

3. Training for management

The importance of training for management was emphasized by many in the research, especially by those who had had considerable experience of secular employment. All clergy need training to manage their individual task in such a diffuse job. If management training were given at each stage, those who become team rectors, archdeacons and bishops would not face time-consuming training once they were appointed, illustrated by the archdeacon's letter in Chapter 18, III, and the replies.

4. Conflict management

Conflict of all sorts, and problems in dealing with it, were constantly mentioned in the interviews. Training in conflict management is seldom emphasized and would be an important part of training generally.

5. Senior laity and training

A complete reassessment could be made of the contribution senior laity could make to ongoing training at each level.

Funding for training within dioceses is limited but input from individual laity, framed within an overall training plan, could greatly enhance clergy performance without incurring high costs. Such training would also help clergy to keep up to date on current thinking both theologically and practically.

6. Consultation and supervision

If 'all other caring professions' have found it necessary to take this issue seriously, the Church may need to reassess its approach. Again, this not only provides support for clergy but also protects the public. Like other professionals, without consultation clergy may become stuck with one particular view of a problem, or may not address an issue, to the detriment of all concerned. For many professions this is done in a small group meeting regularly with a supervisor or consultant. Members then learn not only from discussing their own issues but also from discussion of issues brought by other members.

The distinction between supervision and consultation is that supervisors would normally be in a line management position. Consultants, in this context, provide this professional facility but responsibility for decisions about a situation discussed remains with the individual. This would mean qualified laity could take that role and clergy would still have freedom to exercise their own judgement within appropriate guidelines.

7. Job description, job applications and references

Standard outlines for job descriptions could be drawn up at national level to ensure that essential information is given to applicants. Each parish could, of course, give additional information according to its circumstances.

Theological colleges could equip students to be much more rigorous in teasing out the implications of job descriptions. Training in handling interviews is also important for incumbents, especially as the system of open application and equal opportunities has been introduced since some clergy were ordained.

Agreed outlines for references that include basic information required for ordination candidates by theological colleges and for clergy posts could also be standardized. A consistent system for dealing with 'difficult issues' in references, like debt or affairs, could also be introduced. Candidates would then know from the start of their training how these would be managed.

When clergy consider and apply for jobs, this was shown in the data to have a profound effect on all family members. The Leadership Group recommended the important provision of debriefing for unsuccessful candidates.

8. Financial advice and monitoring

Finance is always a sensitive and personal issue but, as we have seen, the level of stipend affects the family's financial position for all the years of ordination. Three issues need to be addressed:

- Ongoing financial advice from lay professional consultants, beginning at selection, could help families make more informed decisions, especially about dealing with housing. This could include managing any funds which might be inherited at a later stage, with the need for future housing in mind.
- If dioceses have to provide additional assistance or cover debt, specific questions need to be asked at each stage about the family's short-term and long-term financial health and management. This could be done as part of the ongoing financial advice above and provide confidentiality.
- A confidential financial help-line through which clergy could seek advice could prevent the accumulation of debt, which was of great concern to the Leadership Group. Otherwise the 'ideal' and personal embarrassment could prevent even a small debt being addressed until it is out of control.
- An issue to be borne in mind, as the families indicated, is that extra spending may be a response to stress, so debt may be a cry for help.

9. Preparing parishes for a curate

The College Principal recommended much more careful preparation of parishes to receive a curate in order to protect 'the most vulnerable group of clergy, new curates and their families'. The data suggests several ways in which this could be done:

- Comprehensive and ongoing training for training vicars and their churchwardens to be compulsory.
- Curates, especially more mature ordinands, to be treated with respect as trained and competent professional colleagues who are learning a new role, rather than as the untrained students of the past. Most will already have had considerable experience in their home churches as lay members.
- Clear guidance for the curate's role to be provided, including the importance of an uninterrupted full day off each week. The guidelines could be shared with congregations to prevent unrealistic expectations.
- Regular monitoring of the curate's contract/job description between vicar and curate.
- Curates housing should meet agreed standards of size, decoration and cleanliness before the curate takes up the post.
- Curates housing is the responsibility of the parish but curates' terms and conditions of service are the responsibility of the diocese. Their housing should be monitored by the diocese, therefore, to protect them and their families.

Some guidelines exist at present for all of these issues, but vary widely. These would only be effective if there were a system for monitoring and reporting back to college principals and bishops or whoever holds responsibility.

10. Preparing clergy housing

Tighter controls of the preparation and management of all clergy housing could address a long-standing issue of stress for clergy families. The house is in fact part of their 'remuneration'. Unless external monitoring is in place, churchwardens or even individual parishioners may decide what is necessary or appropriate, using their own criteria.

11. Health and the 'working week'

The Leadership Group's comment that the working week should be reassessed could be reviewed. Clergy in some parishes have had an extra day's 'leave' in months that do not have a Bank Holiday, for example. Some attempt to have a five and a half day week when possible. Given all that the clergy and families said about pressure on their time, this may seem unrealistic, but if clergy are to have more of a training role in future, this could be a stage when change could be introduced. This could also address the significant amount of ill health reported by our clergy families.

12. Discipline and pastoral care

The dilemma for bishops of trying to provide both discipline and pastoral care needs to be discussed and clarified. There were issues that clergy or their families might want to discuss at an intermediate level without concerning the archdeacon or bishop. A system to enable this to happen in addition to current structures is urgently needed, to reduce stress for the families and again to protect the leadership from unnecessary interruption.

Throughout their discussions both Groups recommended a system for monitoring families in difficult areas. Remembering the difficulties couples experienced in 'acknowledging anything' for all the reasons discussed, it would be vital for any system to be proactive, and personal contact ensured for it to be effective. If for any reason it was difficult to make contact, follow-up enquiries would be essential, in case the lack of response indicated depression or withdrawal for either of the individuals.

The families and Groups suggested that often the families' concerns were put together and labelled as personal problems, so the families were then seen as not coping. A key point would be to separate the work issues from personal ones and provide support and encouragement accordingly.

All these Recommendations would contribute significantly to the need for a 'Sea Change' emphasized by the American research projects discussed in Chapter 4. They would also move towards the mutuality of care recommended by the Groups in all three interviews and the reciprocal care and concern the families anticipated from within the Church as a whole.

21 A Final Reflection for the Whole Church

We are indebted to all who took part for enabling us to do such in-depth research with so many families over an extended period of time. Research of this nature speaks for itself as we listen to the voices of those involved. Its wide range presents strong indicators of the joys and dilemmas of different sections of the Church. It also highlights particular issues that may need to be addressed urgently because of their widespread implications and the stress they cause. Inevitably the Reference Groups provided more individual perspectives, but the spread of representation within the Groups gives a broad base to their comments.

At the outset we included families who were *not* seeking help for difficulties in order to understand the issues facing families in the general course of clergy family life. In view of the Reference Group's many concerns, two questions remain.

- What would a fuller picture be, had those experiencing difficulties been included?

And the Leadership Group's question:

- 'Who is solving the problem?'

If the whole story for each family could have been told, the full extent of the families' faith and commitment would have been revealing. Their plea for a matching commitment from the church echoes throughout the book.

The laity have an increasing part to play. Their encouragement as well as their skills in training and leadership could be invaluable, particularly at this critical time of change. Many comparisons were made during the research. If all church members and the clergy could consider the overall context of a situation, and resist the temptation to make comparisons and criticisms, this would make a significant difference to clergy families and the life of the church. Again our recommendations have come from the data and need to be read in conjunction with the dilemmas. Other issues raised in the section on dilemmas, for which possible 'solutions' were not put forward by the Groups or the families, need further thought and action by those with specific responsibility and expertise.

Resources for Clergy Families

The main charities offering support to clergy and clergy families are listed below. Further details of the range of help they can provide is given on their websites:

1. The Society of Mary and Martha Caring for People in Ministry
   www.sheldon.uk.com
   www.clergyforum.org.uk
2. St Luke's Hospital for the Clergy
   www.stluke@stlukeshospital.org.uk
3. Sons of the Clergy/Friends of the Clergy
   www.clergycharities.org.uk

In addition help and advice is available from:

4. Diocesan Directors of Pastoral Care, and
5. Diocesan Directors of Education,

whose contact details can be found on the websites of the relevant diocese/s. Most dioceses now also have a clergy counselling helpline

6. Westminster Pastoral Foundation
   www.wpf.org.uk
7. Broken Rites
   www.brokenrites.org.uk.